REVOLUTION AND RESTORATION

IDIOM INVENTING WRITING THEORY

Jacques Lezra and Paul North, series editors

REVOLUTION AND RESTORATION

THE POLITICS OF ANACHRONISM

MASSIMILIANO TOMBA

Fordham University Press *New York 2025*

For EU safety / GPSR concerns: Mare Nostrum Group B.V., Mauritskade 21D, 1091 GC Amsterdam, The Netherlands, gpsr@mare-nostrum.co.uk

Library of Congress Cataloging-in-Publication Data available online at https://catalog.loc.gov.

Printed in the United States of America

27 26 25 5 4 3 2 1

First edition

CONTENTS

PREFACE

The past returns, bringing with it nightmares, morbid phenomena, possibilities, and hopes. It is a persistent shadow that not only haunts but also illuminates the potential futures woven into its fabric. The return of the past is not merely a revival of what has been but a fertile ground where the dreams of yesterday merge with the aspirations of tomorrow.

In May 2023, when *Revolution and Restoration* was essentially finished, I was invited to a conference in Berlin. There I heard about an exhibition at the Deutsches Historisches Museum. The title was "Roads Not Taken. Oder: Es hätte auch anders kommen können." I found the title intriguing. The exhibition offered fourteen turning points in German history, from 1989 going back to 1848. In order to present German history in a new light, the exhibition displayed possible scenarios and events that could have happened. What new light? The light of the present through a legitimizing reverse teleology. The implicit question that resonated from the themes of the exhibition can be rephrased as follows: What roads were fortunately not taken so that humanity could sidestep a communist future? What other roads allowed Germany to escape the "warm war" that divided North and South Korea? What paths were avoided to prevent the apocalypse of the atomic bomb? These counterfactual histories show what might have occurred had history taken a different course, thereby giving the inhabitants of the present the comforting illusion that they have avoided catastrophes far greater than the evils that may afflict them today.

Counterfactual stories are all the rage in a present that seems frozen, devoid of real alternatives, and destined to march almost inexorably toward a new catastrophe: climate catastrophe. Hence the need to write histories of what might have been. Through counterfactual analysis, historians and researchers seek to mobilize a new chain of reasoning to question both past futures and possible futures. The barriers between objective and subjective, real and fictional, and so on are challenged by the author's counterfactual gesture. This is exemplified by critical fabulation, which presses at the limits of the case file and speculates about what might have been in order to imagine moments of possibility.

However different, the stories of roads not taken express a common sense of despair about a present in which one is stuck. Authors and readers process this despair by convincing themselves that things could have been worse, or by self-gratification through the creation of a past of possibilities, or, again, by attributing voice and agency to victims or characters from the past. This historiographic genre should be interpreted as a symptom. In the stagnant, dead-end present, where the individual feels entrapped, critical scholars extract new possibilities from within themselves, much like Baron Munchausen hoisting himself out of the swamp by his own pigtail. This subjectivism represents a contemporary iteration of idealism, where the self becomes both the moral judge and savior, fashioning an escape from the inertia of current reality.

This raises the question: How is it possible to free the present from its inertia? The reasons for this inertia are manifold. They have to do with the way we think about history and the concepts we use to shape reality. The notion of progress, with its unilinear conception of time, is no longer convincing and has lost its hermeneutic power. The future, imagined without new concepts, becomes an extension of the present. Futurity without true change. To overcome this impasse, thinkers such as Daniel Bensaïd, Peter Osborne, Susan Buck-Morss, Gary Wilder, and Harry Harootunian have worked on alternative conceptions of historical time. In different ways and forms they can be seen as part of a tradition of thought that includes thinkers such as Lefebvre, Fanon, Sartre, Bloch, Benjamin, and Marx. *Revolution and Restoration* situates itself within this tradition to explore the clash between historical layers that are co-present yet temporally distinct.

Revolution and Restoration examines concrete possibilities that emerge not from the imaginative pen of a thinker but from the energy generated when incompatible legal and economic structures come into conflict in social and political movements. It is about extracting normativity from practices understood as theory in action. It involves a kind of exemplary or epistemic normativity that emerges in social and political practices. These constitute the living archive of an alternative path to the exhausted one of today's political and critical theory. In these practices, new political concepts are forged to break free from the constraints of the present and shape a different future. This is an urgent task. Indeed, the sense of being stuck in the present generates an angry energy that provides the impetus for both historical and contemporary fascist movements. They draw their strength from the friction between nonsynchronous temporal layers. These frictions are politicized and ultimately synchronized, channeling the discontent into what Harry Harootunian calls a global fascist imaginary. The opposite of fascist politics is not to be found in the celebration of progress or the reiteration of exhausted liberal-democratic dogmas but in a new relationship to the past that sees anachronisms as fields of possibilities. These are not aleatory possibilities floating in a void. Possibilities for their own sake are futile. What we seek are concrete possibilities, deeply rooted in present struggles and social movements. They represent breaches within the present, yet they are also imbued with a sense of direction toward a different future.

The compass that was supposed to guide humanity toward a better future has lost its needle. People orient themselves as best they can, thus leading to the fragmentation of the present. *Revolution and Restoration* addresses this fractured reality and works with the theory in action that has emerged in recent political and social movements. It seeks to develop new concepts that emerge from the collision of asynchronous and incompatible legal and social structures, with the aim of illuminating alternative political frameworks for the present.

Istanbul, August 2024

POSTSCRIPTUM

For the most part, this book was conceived and written between 2018 and 2023. Rereading it now, many diagnoses concerning the rise of new forms of authoritarianism have gained greater relevance and, unfortunately, confirmation. Yet the book's main intervention remains the same: how to transform unfortunate circumstances into an opportunity to spark and steer change.

The authoritarian implosion of a growing number of states is not merely the result of botched elections; it is a symptom of the crisis of the modern state and its inability to govern phenomena whose complexity far exceeds the constitutional mechanisms originally designed to regulate them. The crisis is not the result of attacks against liberal institutions; those attacks should be understood as symptoms of a deeper malaise. Yet, we must be careful not to confuse symptoms with causes.

The present condition might be described as a restoration without a prior revolution, but it is also a restoration without revolutionary movements. It is not only the strength of such movements that elicits authoritarian backlashes but also their weakness, which manifests in their inability to contain the latent authoritarianism inscribed in the very architecture of the modern Leviathan.

Today, the state of emergency has once again become the rule. But there is a key difference. In the recent past, violations of domestic and international law still required some form of justification. They took place in the name of real or alleged emergencies. Sovereignty was violated in the name of human rights and humanitarian interventions; fundamental rights were suspended in the war against terrorism. Today, however, international law and the *jus belli* are drawn into a permanent state of suspension, signaling a transition toward a new world order yet to be defined. State sovereignty, now outliving its own logic, is sustained by the intensification of its most primordial functions—particularly at the borders—and by the fluid redefinition of internal and external enemies. The logic of the border, with its vicious mixture of the legal and the illegal, is increasingly permeating the social fabric of states. Deportations are on the rise. New categories of crime are being invented. Defense spending is increasing. The trade war has already begun. Everything suggests that a new world war is in the making.

In this conjuncture, the governed are left behind; they are excluded from centers of decision making. Fed up with their exclusion, they are ready to exclude others to simulate their inclusion within the state. Nationalism reemerges. The growing legal, political, and economic indeterminacy demands management through rapid and decisive action. As a result, the authoritarian form of the state appears to be the most suitable for the task. To believe that the current crisis can be slowed down or controlled by merely changing those in power is hopeful but, unfortunately, futile. It's like believing you can take control of a ship, only to discover that it's on autopilot and has no manual controls.

The crisis runs deep and must be addressed from the very foundations of the political, economic, and legal edifice of modernity. The crisis has also affected educational institutions, which have become a battleground—a terrain to be conquered by both sides of the political spectrum. The diagnosis of the present is undoubtedly bleak. However, it has always been philosophy's task to offer prognoses. Fulfilling this task requires a careful investigation of the past, as well as the ability to understand and intervene in the present to bring about a real change of course. I hope that the numerous social and political experiments discussed in this book can offer us precisely that: By recombining revolution and restoration, they open the present to new, concrete possibilities.

Santa Cruz, April 2025

REVOLUTION AND RESTORATION

The good new is never entirely new. It does not come from an empty hand or from an apparently free-floating head.

—Ernst Bloch

INTRODUCTION
THE WORK OF ANACHRONISM AND THE CONFIGURATION OF NEW CONCEPTS

There are terms such as natural law, religion, tradition, authority, obligation, and restoration that the "left" has abandoned and that are now almost completely controlled by conservative forces. These terms had, and still have, an emancipatory potential, capable of mobilizing affects and political energy. The natural law tradition has been appropriated by conservative forces to justify the natural right to private property as inherent in the natural order of things and, more recently, to condemn abortion, euthanasia, or gay marriage. There is, however, a different tradition. It is the *ius naturale* mobilized by the peasants to defend common possession; it is the natural right that also inflamed French revolutionaries to operate justice from below;[1] it is the Black natural law tradition recovered by Frederick Douglass, Anna Julia Cooper, W. E. B. Du Bois, and Martin Luther King Jr. It is a tradition that practices natural law as a way of questioning the justice of the existing order and opening up processes of transformation based on a notion of *human* "as exceeding all worldly description."[2]

It was on the basis of the same excess that Olympe de Gouges's feminist project of making women political subjects took shape. In this revolutionary context, terms such as "human rights" and "humanity" were used by women, enslaved people, and the poor to question existing hierarchies and exclusions.[3] Common possession was defended on the basis of natural law from the early Western modern age up to Thomas Spence, who, in *The Restorer of Society*, advocated for the abolition of private ownership of land and the restoration of

1

society to its natural state, i.e., small bodies or parishes, in which land would belong to the inhabitants in an equal manner.[4]

It is a political and theoretical disaster that today these same terms are attacked or dismissed by forces that like to present themselves as radical and in favor of social and political change. Tradition is qualified in opposition to progress, common obligations in opposition to individual rights, restoration in opposition to revolution, religion in opposition to secularism.[5] The result of these oppositions is twofold. On the one hand, they have provided conservative forces with a variety of emotionally and politically charged concepts. On the other, these oppositions temporalize these same terms so that tradition, religion, and restoration appear regressive in the face of progressivism, secularism, and revolution.

To defend different ways of life, numerous insurgents have appealed to local authority, religion, tradition, past institutions, local customs, and alternative forms of obligation. So-called progressive factions have disparaged them as anachronisms. Conversely, reactionary groups have romanticized them to reinstate direct forms of control, exclusion, and novel hierarchies. Progressive and reactionary forces are as complementary as the positive and negative polarity of an electrical circuit. The way out of this cyclical dynamic can be indicated by a political practice that reconfigures and produces concepts in the tension between legal, social, and economic forms.

* * *

The state form that emerged in the fifteenth and sixteenth centuries, theorized by Hobbes and Locke, and developed into modern constitutional forms between the eighteenth and nineteenth centuries, rested on the political participation of a minority of free and property-owning citizens. The representative model allowed for the expansion of the represented base, the *demos*, into a constitutional structure in which a narrow oligarchy ruled the nation. This model was subject to a constant balancing of the relationship between the ruling, governing class and the governed. Extending the right to vote to the governed changed the organic composition of the ruling class but did not in any real way change the form of the state, which remained based on the govern of a narrow oligarchy of representatives. The question today is: How much democracy can the modern liberal-democratic state endure? In other words, can this representative form adapt to the massive entry of large segments of the population into the political machine? In the early 1900s, the irruption of the masses coincided with the formation of new political parties, mass parties, and the polarization between fascism and communism. Parties became internally disciplined structures, and parliament became the forum where decisions already made in party headquarters were made public. The postwar years in Europe constituted a social-democratic interregnum in which class conflict was channeled into a dynamic of democratization and extension of rights. This interregnum has ended. The extension of suffrage has generated indifference. The number of those who do not go to the polls, despite having the right to do so, is constantly growing. Mass parties have given way to populist movements and formations through which the governed try to regain the floor and challenge the ruling class and its oligarchic privileges. The masses today are not acting on the basis of party organization or a political program; rather, they are propelled by resentment, anger, and dissatisfaction with a political power they perceive as increasingly remote and for too long in the hands of the same elite. In the absence of politically directed change, the masses opt for change of any kind. It does not matter if the new populist leaders are billionaires. What matters is that they share with the masses a disgust with the old oligarchy.

The formal democracy of the modern representative state operates on behalf of the *demos*, but the *demos* must remain dormant and be *re-presented* by a governing elite. Its *presence* disturbs the functioning of the old representative machine and is always in excess.[6] The "democratic excess" was a term used derogatorily by Robespierre. In 1793, during a session of the National Convention, participants discussed a petition by primary assemblies demanding the right and authority to convene spontaneously. Robespierre not only spearheaded its rejection but also argued that such a right "would destroy all forms of government and, by excess of democracy (*par excès de démocratie*), overthrow national sovereignty."[7] The democratic excess to which Robespierre objected was the institutional practice of assemblies of the poor and women, the questioning of the absolute individual right to property, the authority of assemblies to recall representatives according to the imperative mandate model, and the practice of political citizenship as forms of direct participation in popular assemblies. In the same year, Condorcet had expressed his opposition to the revocation of the mandataries by the sections and the practice of the imperative mandate, desired by the sans-culottes and *enragés*, because it would have led to the destruction of the unity of will and action of the nation.[8] Both Condorcet's balanced approach to democracy and the excess of democracy, which aimed to restore and renew the political fabric of society, were contrasted by the democracy claimed in the name of the people and the centralization of power in the hands of the Convention. This led to the logic of Terror, which was not an expression of excess but rather a reaction against it. On February 5, 1794, Robespierre stated: "Democracy is not a state in which the people, continually assembled, regulates by itself all public affairs; even less is it a state in which one hundred thousand fractions of the people . . . would decide the fate of the whole of society."[9]

The democratic excess challenged by Robespierre during the Revolution took shape in the rearticulation of a dispersed sovereignty in which assemblies exercised constant control over representatives. The pluralization of *kratos* changes both the notion of *demos* and the concept of politics. Reviving the medieval institution of the imperative mandate, Jean Varlet advocated sovereignty to the primary assemblies and sections in which the people actually assembled and discussed, controlled and tabulated orders to the mandataries. He challenged the grammar of representation: "Deputies, you will no longer be our representatives, you will be our mandataries, our organ."[10] During the French Revolution, the revolutionary progressive temporality was confronted with the restorative temporality of institutional structures such as the imperative mandate, the limitation of ownership, and corporate forms of common deliberation. These forms were judged as residues of the Ancien Régime, regressive phenomena, "unconstitutional, derogatory to liberty and the declaration of the rights of man,"[11] and therefore had to be wiped out.

In 1792, Pauline Léon, who was close to the group of the *enragés*, claimed revolutionary citizenship for women, including the right to bear arms. Women were acting as political citizens beyond the legal recognition of their citizenship. In March 1792, a deputy of the Legislative Assembly, Dehaussy-Robecourt, replied by saying that if the petition of Léon were honored, "the order of nature would be inverted (*intervertir l'ordre de la nature*)."[12] Nevertheless, women continued to join the army. But despite their heroic examples, on April 30, 1793, the National Convention decreed that all women currently serving in the military would be immediately discharged and sent home with a modest travel allowance. The attack on women's political citizenship culminated during the Terror, under the leadership of the Jacobins. On October 30, 1793, Jean-Baptiste Amar, speaking for the Committee of Public Security, proposed a decree to suppress all women's political clubs: "Should women exercise political rights and get mixed up in the affairs of government? . . . We can respond in general no. . . . Secondly, should women gather together in political associations? . . . No, because they would be obliged to sacrifice more important cares to which nature calls them. The private functions (*fonctions privée*) to which women are destined by nature itself follow from the general order of society. The clubs and popular societies of women, under whatever denomination, are prohibited."[13] To bottle up the democratic excess and put the *demos* back to sleep, it was necessary to depoliticize and differentiate society from the political state. Women were relegated to the private sphere and deprived of their public-political life. These distinctions were then frozen by being elevated to the status of natural determinations of the social order.

The binaries of public/private, political/social, and others are specifically modern and were produced as weapons for political purposes: to depoliticize and neutralize social conflicts. For example, religion, the basis not only of confessional wars but also of millenarian uprisings, has been depoliticized through the political/social pair and, through the public/private pair, has been confined to the private sphere. Here everyone is free to profess the faith he or she prefers, to the extent that it is politically inert. Similarly, knowledge and behaviors that do not conform to the dominant rationality are free to proliferate in the private sphere insofar as they do not undermine in any way the edifice of the state, which, firmly established on other deeper levels of binary oppositions, tolerates them insofar as it depoliticizes them. To put it in different terms, one could say that the constant function of the political state is the depoliticization of the social. This demarcation has not been established once and for all. The state can redefine what is tolerable based on new oppositions that individuals articulate through moral, cultural, religious, and economic arguments. Marx had grasped the process well—the "political revolution"—which "destroyed all the estates, corporations, guilds and privileges . . . *abolished the political character of civil society*"[14] and gave rise to the modern individual, the "*unpolitical* man,"[15] whose life was split into a long series of binaries such as *citoyen* and *bourgeois*, public and private, political and civil, state and social, communal and selfish, spiritual and material (to which we might add male and female). For the young Marx, these divisions, which were the result of the political revolution, could be sublated by the social revolution that had at its center the human being no longer split but reconciled with its kind. Marx's solution was still Hegelian in that he saw the supersession of the contradiction of the present in a superior historical level to be realized.

My method of working, which remains in the materialist tradition initiated by Marx, shows that there are political events that can destabilize these demarcations and produce new concepts. However, those repeated challenges have also generated a political and theoretical reaction that has often resulted in a solidification and naturalization of the binaries. The peasants, for having defended legal and proprietary systems incompatible with those of the dominant modernity, were defined as internal savages to be colonized.[16] The laboring insurgents, for

6

INTRODUCTION

having attacked a system of exploitation and defended the collective rights of associations, were qualified as barbarians, hostile to the new rights of man and at war against civilization.[17] Women, for having defended their natural right to enter the political sphere and having attacked an order structured on the division between public and private, which confines women to the household, have been displayed as monstrous and pathologized.[18] To the extent that the instability of the modern political form is exposed, the reaction is the reconsolidation and naturalization of the binaries that give the appearance of some stability. The dominant tradition of political theory works to generate stability by guarding the boundaries of sovereignty against the democratic excess.

Although "democratic excess" was coined as a negative description, my aim is to reappropriate it to show how it reshapes property, political participation, and citizenship. Rejecting the binary of chaos versus order, I show how political practices from below that appear as an "excess" of democracy and thus detrimental to it can in fact offer the possibility of an alternative order that goes beyond some of the impasses of modern, representative national states. The "democratic excess" may challenge numerous binary oppositions on which the edifice of the modern political order has been built. These binaries give stability to the edifice and for this reason, in times of crisis, their polemical virulence intensifies. The democratic excess undoes these binaries and makes the edifice unstable. This is why it causes concern among both conservatives and liberals. When, in democratic excess, anachronistic institutions are reactivated and reconfigured to reshape the present, the opposition between the regressive and the progressive, between anachronism and actuality, is also called into question.

* * *

Anachronism is a term that generally has a negative value; it denotes the remnant of a previous era, something that, when it exists, is out of harmony with the present. It is an error that consists either in putting a fact too early (*prochronism*) or too late (*parachronism*). If the term "synchronism," which appeared in 1588, indicated coherence or agreement between different events happening at the same time,[19] then the term "anachronism," which appeared later in the seventeenth century, indicated an error in the completion of time or in synchronism.

There exists a historical painting, *The Battle of Alexander at Issus*, which contains significant anachronism. Albrecht Altdorfer painted it in 1529 on commission from Duke William IV of Bavaria. In order to represent the Battle of Issus, which occurred in 333 BCE, Altdorfer consulted Curtis Rufus so that he could stage the exact number of combatants, dead, and prisoners on both sides. All of these groups are simultaneously present in the painting, as if time were frozen so that the entire battle could be represented. The painting attracted the attention of Reinhart Koselleck, who pointed out how Altdorfer "made conscious use of anachronism" by representing the course of the entire battle.[20] But Koselleck's attention is primarily directed toward another anachronism: the Battle of Issus, with Persians resembling Turks, evokes the Ottoman Empire's first attempt to capture Vienna in the same year as the painting was painted. Koselleck is interested in highlighting the lack of critical historical distance that characterizes Altdorfer's work. To do this, he juxtaposes Altdorfer's experience of historical time with that of Friedrich Schlegel, who, when he came across the painting nearly three hundred years later, called it "the greatest feat of the age of Chivalry."[21] The thesis underlying Koselleck's reflection is that in the centuries that separate Altdorfer from Schlegel, that is, between the Reformation and the French Revolution, "there occurs a temporalization (*Verzeitlichung*) of history."[22] Koselleck's conception of the modern temporalization of history is based on the assumption of the lack of temporalization of historical time in the "premodern." I argue instead that what appears as anachronism or confusion of historical time in the Middle Ages must be understood not in terms of a lack but of different criteria for the temporalization of time.[23] The temporalization to which Koselleck refers operates through a specific modern form of conceptualization of historical material. In the premodern Christian world, as emphasized by Erich Auerbach, "an occurrence on earth signifies not only itself but at the same time another, which it predicts or confirms. . . . The connection between occurrences is not regarded as primarily a chronological or causal development but as a oneness within the divine plan, of which all occurrences are parts and reflections."[24] In the medieval image of historical time, it is as if the world were stretched vertically and from here, from this vertical hierarchy, given order. When the earthly order, its hierarchies, are shaken, the backlash is felt on the vertical divine. For this reason, historically, uprisings intertwined with a proliferation of heretical movements, which, in an attempt to restore the original Christian community, shook the foundations of the medieval hierarchical order.

Different temporalizations of history continue to coexist in modernity. The references to the original Christian community made by Winstanley, Müntzer, and Savonarola do not indicate a desire to return to a bygone era. Nor are they merely rhetorical. The reference to origin is such that it exceeds the present time and introduces a rupture. Origin does not lie at the beginning of time but outside of it. Like God's *aeternitas*, in the origin, the present and the past collide. What is at stake is another temporal dimension in tension with the one that is dominant in the present. It is possible to draw an analogy with contemporary indigenous conceptions of time. In the Aymara conception of history, the past is not something dead or inert. Rather, from it, the hope of a different future can be nurtured, "so that the past can be regenerated in the future."[25] In this sense, the temporality of its return should be understood as "the recovery of the course of our history," that is, a history free from colonial dominion.[26] It is not a matter of resetting five hundred years of colonial history to zero but of reconfiguring it in the present from the past. In the words of Silvia Rivera Cusicanqui, "the restoration of the cosmic order—which the idea of a linear and progressive historical time refuses to understand, if not as a 'turning back the wheel of history'—can also be understood through the notion of *nayrapacha* . . . : past, but not just any vision of the past, rather a 'past-as-future,' that is, as a renewal of time-space. A past capable of renewing the future, of overturning the situation that has been lived out."[27] The work of anachronism in this book should also be understood in a similar way. The overturning of the temporal order, of the railway sequence of past, present, and future, makes room for restorative dynamics capable of modifying the present by freeing futures imprisoned in the past.

Modern unilinear time operates as a synchronizing device with respect to other temporalities. This means that different legal, social, and economic structures are arranged on the historical timeline so that what is out of sync with respect to the dominant representation of the present is *eo ipso* qualified as residual or delayed. What characterizes the unilinearity of modern historical time is not the denial of different temporalities. It is easy to think of the co-presence of multiple temporalities because we constantly experience them. Instead, unilinearity functions as a synchronization and legitimation of actual processes that conform to the present temporality and forms of life and law that are defined as anachronistic. This is where the normative force of the present comes from.

Synchronization operates on the basis of concrete processes and institutions. The state, through its apparatuses and institutions, imposes a historical narrative, a calendar of national celebrations, and a homogeneous legal system that pulverizes juridical "anachronisms." The capitalist mode of production, through the normative and synchronizing temporality of socially necessary labor time, "regulates" the competition among capitals and that between capital and labor force. Marx had captured the overriding character of capitalist time in these terms: "In all forms of society it is a determinate production and its relations which assign every other production and its relations their rank and influence. It is a general illumination in which all other colours are plunged and which modifies their specific tonalities. It is a special ether which defines the specific gravity of everything found in it."[28] Not only the different forms of production but also traditions, identities, and races have taken their own shape in these tensions and cannot be studied independently of these tensions. Here anachronism and its ambiguous character also emerges: delay and residue to be eliminated, or possibility and disruption. Jacques Rancière defined it as "a word, an event, or a signifying sequence that has left 'its' time, and in this way is given the capacity to define completely original points of orientation to carry out leaps from one temporal line to another."[29] The notion of anachrony requires a nonlinear conception of time. It may be useful to think of a topological notion of time, in which, as space is curved, so is time, and distant points on the calendar may be very close together.

Anachronism works in the present as scandalous temporalities, in the exact sense that the term *scandalum* had in Greek, that is, "obstacle" or "stumbling block." However, if it is such, it is only in relation to the dominant or synchronizing temporality. These processes have a history. As early as the fourteenth century in France, the tension between biblical and ritual time and the new time of labor and markets was defined by real clashes. When bells began to be used no longer just to mark time in religious rituals but to command when workers had to start and end working, eating, drinking, and sleeping, workers' "uprisings were subsequently aimed at silencing the *Werkglocke*."[30] Against these uprisings, the nascent state power carried out a crucial function in the synchronization of time, when as early as 1370 Charles V "ordered that all the bells of Paris be regulated by the clock at the Palais-Royal, which tolled the hours and the quarter-hours. The new time thus became the time of the state."[31] This new notion of time also had to be internalized by individuals through institutions and workplaces. E. P. Thompson describes the pedagogy of the new discipline of time in these terms: "The first generation of factory workers were taught by their masters the importance of time; the second generation formed their short-time committees in the ten-hour movement; the third generation struck for overtime or time-and-a-half. They had accepted the categories of their employers and learned to fight back within them. They had learned their lesson, that time is money, only too well."[32] Capitalist time, i.e., socially necessary labor time, asserted itself as a time of new unnatural work rhythms. It became common experience through a long war against customs, usage, and different experiences of time. Synchronization clashed—and clashes—with other temporalities, as can be seen when peasants stole the bells that rang the beginning and end of the working day or when the workers broke the factory clocks that marked the working day. These are historical examples characterized by the conflict between traditional and anachronistic temporalities versus the synchronizing mechanisms of the new capitalist and state time. Both the state and the capitalist mode of production are such syn-chronizing mechanisms. As I have explained elsewhere, both of these dynamics require "not only clocks, but also their synchronization."[33] In the sixteenth cen-tury, the need arose to make clocks accurate; thus the minute hand was added.[34]

These violent dynamics of synchronizations generate friction and tension. E. P. Thompson's analysis of moral economy can be resumed to explore what is produced by the energy that arises in the tension between incompatible legal systems.[35] Thompson's analysis is articulated on at least three levels: There is the contrast with the new political economy of the free market; there is the recourse to the "paternalist model" of market regulation, such as the 1630 *Book of Orders* to which the rioters appealed; there is the direct action of the crowd, which, sometimes claiming its own legitimacy from the old paternalist model, enforced market control through disciplined insurrections that exhibited patterns of be-havior. Forms of "rebellions" emerge that, however violent, were governed by another legality. A clash of legal systems emerges where the crowd does not act "against" but in accordance with traditions and customs of and obligations to another legal system. From this perspective, the very term "resistance" should be used with caution. Its modern meaning is steeped in a liberal perspective in that it is immediately linked to morality and individual rights. It is the opposite of the classic *ius resistentiae*, based on natural law, that is, the obligation to defend and restore an existing legal form from the unjust violation of the tyrant. The field of forces can be portrayed as follows: On the one hand, customs and tradi-tions are reactivated and reconfigured as a source of authority and justification for popular demands. On the other, the new laissez faire model celebrated by modern philosophers and economists is constructed *polemically* against both the old paternalist model of market regulation and the insurgent moment or the crowd's moral economy. The laissez faire theory, like every theory, was born on a battlefield and *bears the traces of its opponents*. My method works in that battlefield, without taking the point of view of the new legal and disciplinary system and without romanticizing the old order and tradition. It is a question of showing how in the reactivation of anachronistic customs and traditions, their reinvention is at stake. And not only their reinvention but also the configuration of new concepts.

* * *

Concepts are temporalizing devices. Conceptualization that operates accord-ing to a unilinear conception of historical time periodizes and orders historical material into successive stages. This happens whenever the prefix "pre-" is used to characterize pre-modern, pre-state, pre-capitalist, etc. forms. By ordering the past, the work of concepts extends to the present and the future so that concepts themselves become heralds of historical trends. It is no exaggeration to say that this conceptualization, as it operates behind the back of the historian and theorist, is a form of unconscious ideology. The very same is implicit in the definition of the Jacobin Terror as *dérapage* in the work of François Furet, of fascism as a parenthesis in Benedetto Croce's work, or of Nazism as an unfortunate accident in Friedrich Meinecke. If those historical events can be defined, and studied, in those ways, it means that a "normal" course of history and politics that coincides with the liberal democratic state is assumed. This is an aspect of the philosophy of history underlying those historical reconstructions. This is what I call reverse teleology.

It is important to understand how the reverse teleology works and implicitly operates in the conceptualization of historical material. On the basis of this reverse teleology, Hegel created the historical-philosophical itinerary of modern consciousness. In doing so, he replaced the authority of tradition, taken up by the Romantics, with the authority of historical progress. When he dwells on the clash between Creon and Antigone, between the human law of the city and the divine law of the dead, the whole story is constructed from the point of view of the reverse teleology. It is the outcome of that conflict that shapes the story of Antigone conceptualized in *Phenomenology of Spirit*. The result is the establishment of Roman-modern law, the new form of universality that confines divine law to the private sphere. The individual no longer has value as a member of a family or community but only as an individual: "Individuality has been shattered into a multitude of separate atoms."[36] In this framework, atomization, privatization, and individuality were born as moments of a specific historical-political dynamic.

In presenting the conflict between Antigone and Creon, Hegel was laying out the conflict between customary legal structures and state law in his own time. This was not a matter of philosophical abstraction but of the reception of modern civil law in the General State Laws for the Prussian States, the *Allgemeines Landrecht* (1794), and its tangled relationship to customary law. This was not just a transition from a feudal to a proprietary system but a conflict between legal systems. This conflict, again in 1842, drew Marx's attention when, in an article on the "Debates on the Law on Thefts of Wood," he discussed the new legislative interventions of the Rhineland Diet that considered the poor peasants' custom of collecting dead twigs and fronds in state forests as theft.[37] The clash is between incompatible legal systems, and their opposition cannot be negated, mediated, and eventually elevated to a new level, as happens in Hegelian super-session (*Aufhebung*).

Deep temporal strata are not superseded.[38] They run across the dominant temporal trajectory of modernity and resurface when the energy released by their friction can no longer be contained. Such an image must have been clear to the witnesses of the agrarian rebellions of the Whiteboys between 1760 and 1790: "Property in Ireland resembled the thin soil of volcanic countries spread lightly over subterranean fires."[39] When that thin surface cracked, the freed energy, charged with the memory and tradition of the commons, threatened to blow up existing property relations. A similar energy, charged with memory and legal traditions, emerged in the more recent water war in Cochabamba and in the practices of the Zapatistas in Chiapas.

Reverse teleology is instead the celebration of the surface. It means looking at the past from the point of view of the present, understood as the end of a chain of events that derive their own sense, or even non-sense, from subsequent developments. It is the present or the future, understood as the trend of an epoch, that gives meaning to the past. This teleology allows temporalities that are incompatible with the present to be considered anachronisms, something archaic to be eliminated. In this way, modern concepts express their second fundamental characteristic. Not only do they temporalize historical material, but they are also polemical concepts. European modernity arose by creating America as a blank page of history that Europeans could write from scratch, like in the allegorical illustration by Van der Straet in de Bry's volume *America decima pars* (1619), and in contrast to the Middle Ages, which were negatively qualified as the Dark Ages, in order to produce a self-representation of modernity in light and positive terms.[40] Indeed, modern political theorists and legal scholars have shaped the self-representation of modernity by producing the concept of feudal-ism as a counterconcept.[41] The colonization of the past and the colonization of the globe arose together. The latter operates through a temporalization of geo-graphic space, so that entire areas of the planet are qualified as "backward" and the people who inhabit them as barbarians to be civilized.

Western modernity emerged as a polemical concept in opposition to what preceded it. It is the tabula rasa produced by Cartesian doubt against Aristote-lian tradition and preexisting knowledge, and it is the Hobbesian state of nature conceived against existing legal forms and customs in society. The concept of Western modernity is polemical not only because it took shape through pro-cesses of colonization both within and beyond Europe but also because it was constituted as an epoch that produces epochs by temporalizing and periodizing differences. When qualitatively different political, legal, and economic forms are conceptualized, they are also processed and periodized so that they can be ordered into historical-temporal stages, lags, or historical residues. Modern concepts constantly carry out this processualization, to the point of becoming normative in terms of historical direction. Colonialism operates in accordance with this grammar.

Today, many postcolonial and decolonial discourses do not escape this polemical conceptualization when they contrast a monolithic Western and colonial Europe with the oppressed and silenced inhabitants of the colonial world. This opposition erases the history of colonialism within Europe itself.[42] The German peasants of 1525, the Diggers of 1649, the Communards of 1871, and many other insurgents of Western modernity defended other legal systems and property relations against the dominant modernity. In doing so, they recalled and refunctioned local forms of self-government, traditional customs and practices, the Bible, and medieval institutions. They paid a heavy price for standing in the way of "Western civilization." They were inferiorized, pathologized, and racialized. To erase their history and display Europe as a monolithic colonial bloc means to massacre again those already massacred. It means accepting the self-representation of the dominant modernity and reproducing its original gesture. It means opposing Western modernity by means of an intensified polemical opposition, this time of the colonized against colonial Europe and its structures of thought. This opposition was often the basis for anticolonial wars, the outcome of which paved the way for an internal colonialism in which the new ruling classes imposed legal forms, constitutional structures, and civil codes borrowed from the West and introduced the new national economies into the world market. This is what happened in the Haitian revolutions and in countless revolutions that resulted in desperate attempts to catch up with the dominant Western modernity. To avoid this repetition compulsion, another way of thinking and politics is needed. Other concepts are needed.

* * *

New concepts take shape in concrete historical events characterized by tensions between incompatible systems. New concepts are not the result of a Hegelian *Aufhebung*. They emerge in uprisings and social and political movements. They are not produced by some neologism of academics and scholars. Neologisms are like a coat of paint on an old, moth-eaten piece of furniture: They give the illusion of newness. They cover up more than they help to understand and innovate.

The creation of concepts as a task of philosophy was explored by Deleuze and Guattari in *What Is Philosophy?* According to the French authors, the creation of concepts is the work of *conceptual personae*, like Plato's Socrates. An example of creation is also the Cartesian *cogito*. It arises from presuppositions, and its specific presupposition is that "everyone can think."[43] It should be added that this formula is already polemical. To claim that "everyone can think" is to attack the old Aristotelian assumption that someone is excluded from the *logos*. This is where history comes in. The assumption that everyone can think comes from concrete battles in which the excluded, the slaves, the plebeians, the poor, and women challenged their exclusion by practically questioning the justice of the existing order based on their exclusion. They did not ask permission to participate in the discourse of what is right. They burst into the *logos* by imposing a new discourse of justice on the dominant. The equality that underlies the assumption that "everyone can think" is produced by concrete historical battles, by countless *jacqueries* and peasant uprisings in the fifteenth and sixteenth centuries. It is in these uprisings that a new configuration of concepts and counterconcepts takes place. This is what is missing in Deleuze and Guattari's philosophical analysis. When Descartes assumes the egalitarian principle of *cogito* and Hobbes presupposes the natural equality of individuals, they introduce into philosophy what can no longer be excluded: the cry for equality. But in doing so, by subsuming equality into a new philosophical discourse, they neutralize the subversive charge of equality by overturning it into universal obedience to an order founded according to *more geometrico*. Hobbes is clear in this regard: Everyone can understand the *ratio* of the law, and therefore everyone is bound to obey the authority of the sovereign if he or she does not want to fall back into a state of nature characterized by uncertainty and the constant risk of being killed. The result is simple and universally understandable: It is *rational* to obey the law in order to preserve the civilized state; it is *irrational* to disobey and risk a relapse into the state of nature.

An example of the polemical origin of modern concepts can also be found in the theological concepts developed in the Lutheran Reformation. Luther's interpretations of Romans 13:1—"Let every person be subject to the governing authorities; for there is no authority except from God, and those authorities that exist have been instituted by God"—is polemical. Luther interpreted this formula to justify unconditional obedience to the princes *against* the insurgent theology of the peasants, who instead appealed to godly law and God's authority to challenge new forms of power, private property, and servitude.[44] Similarly, Luther separated the divine realm from the secular realm to neutralize the appeal to Scripture as a source of authority for judging the actions of the princes and transforming the world. Lutheran theology, celebrated by Hegel as introducing the modern principle of individual freedom into the world, is a polemical machine built with weaponized concepts forged in the war against the peasantry.

One has to look at the countless revolts that took place between the fifteenth and sixteenth centuries to understand both the configuration of modern concepts and their polemical nature. The merit of Koselleck's work lies in his demonstration of the polemical nature of modern concepts. He defined these concepts in terms of asymmetric counterconcepts but erred in elevating these polemical structures to forms that are almost metaphysical and found in every historical moment.[45] Instead, their polemical nature must be seen as derived from historical conflict, that is, their use in terms of weaponized concepts to legitimize the winning trajectory, delegitimize the defeated trajectories, and neutralize alternative possibilities.

Attempting to disable the polemical nature of concepts would be a futile exercise. Rather, it is a matter of using their polemical energy in a different way. While the clashes of the early modern age remain significant for the violence in which the concepts still celebrated in the dominant canon took shape, the configuration of new concepts should be understood as an ongoing process that takes place in the clash between mutually incompatible social and legal structures. In *Revolution and Restoration*, I work with the innovative character of the reactivation of anachronistic structures and obligations, whether they are communal, traditional, religious, or related to premodern institutions. These reactivations are possible because these anachronistic structures have not been left behind in the march of progress along a single historical-temporal line. Instead, they coexist as overlapping layers.

* * *

If modern concepts determine their own identity by opposing counterconcepts, my work aims to show the configuration of new concepts that takes place in the political tension between incompatible systems. Going back to the conflict between Antigone and Creon, it is not a matter of standing up for the human law of the city against the divine law of the dead, or the other way around. Much less is it about taking a stand for their supersession. It is a matter of positioning oneself in that tension as it is a force field. It is useful to recall the tragedy of *Antigone* not through the lens of Hegel but through that of his youthful friend Friedrich Hölderlin. For him, "the possible (*das Mögliche*), which enters into reality as reality dissolves, it acts, and brings about both the sensation of dissolution and the memory of what is dissolved."[46] It is this dynamic that would characterize an authentically tragic language. The possible makes itself felt when the real loses its grip on the living. The possible enters reality, provokes the recollection of what is dissolving and its antecedents, and, in the tension between dissolution and recollection, directs the formation of a new temporal order. It is the disruptive force of the possible that opens a cognitive and practical space for the *novum*.

The category of the possible plays a crucial function. Not the "possible" produced ex post from victorious actualizations of past possibilities. Not even the one created by the subjective force of "what if" and "what might have been or said." But the "possible" opened up by the irruption of a new event that, while reactivating elements, traditions, and institutions of the past, also requires a modification of the historical maps that order and give coherence to the relationship between past and present. It is the *practical possible* in which the now draws toward itself pieces of what-has-been to give those pieces new life, while also showing the past as an open arsenal of possible, blocked futures. Making these conflicts between legal trajectories visible means operating in the tension between those systems as one operates in a field of forces and possibilities. It is from this tension and the energy released by the clash between incompatible legal systems that new concepts for politics arise. It is about working with the force-of-invention of concrete agents in the historical battlefield.

From this perspective, the idea of the incompleteness of the past proves crucial to a new historiography and political theory.[47] It is here that "the rigid divisions between future and past thus themselves collapse, unbecome future becomes visible in the past, avenged and inherited, mediated and fulfilled past in the future."[48] But there is no innovation without reference to a tradition. "Traditions, when vital, embody continuities of conflict."[49] Traditions can be rejected in their entirety. Or they can be traversed to work in the tensions inherent in their course. In both cases, traditions function as battlefields. There are structures of repetition, institutions, rituals, and behaviors that operate at deep historical-temporal levels. Concepts contain different temporal layers and history because history runs through them, leaving traces and scars.

Modern concepts order both the prefiguration of the future and, by temporalizing it into epochs and stages, the sense of the past. However, if we consider these concepts not as railroad cars running along the rails of time but rather as forms traversed by time, then the concepts contain historical-temporal sedimentations that can be reordered in particular historical moments marked by social and political tensions. To maintain a parallel with geology, it requires the same energy as an earthquake to reconfigure the order of strata. This energy, produced by the friction between different legal and economic structures, also serves to create spaces of possibility in which new concepts are produced.

Hans Freyer, to whom Koselleck refers, pointed out that history must be understood in geological terms. Just as the earth is the product of a structuring of layers, similarly, history must be represented as the stratification of the historical world in which we live.[50] Taking up Goethe against Hegel, Freyer's image of history is not a succession of epochs, one after another. Rather, it is characterized by the presence of the past in the construction and in the very structure of an epoch. If past and present are co-present as superimposed historical strata, it follows that not only historiography but especially politics always has to do with the synchronicity of the nonsynchronous. This idea, which recurs in both Freyer and Koselleck,[51] had already been used by Ernst Bloch to show how past social and cultural formations continue to flourish in the present and influence its political outcomes.[52] Working with Benjamin and Bloch means thinking about the incompleteness of the past in order to change the present. Benjamin's last text, his theoretical and political testament, is entitled *On the Concept of History*. The title is fitting. For what is at stake is the *concept* of history. That is, a conceptualization that does not submit to the tyranny of the unilinear conception of time. The overturning of the temporal order, of the railway sequence of past, present, and future, makes room for restorative dynamics capable of modifying the present by freeing futures imprisoned in the past.

The concept of democracy, for example, did not develop progressively along the timeline from the Greek *polis* to the modern representative democratic state. It is crisscrossed by history and contains different semantic sediments, which correspond to historical layers of the term "democracy." Making history of the possible means learning to work with concepts differently. When we talk about democracy, we have to abandon the idea of an evolutionary and linear history of the concept of democracy, culminating in the liberal-democratic representative state. Instead, we need to think of a multilayered concept of democracy, in which the concept of the representative democratic state is only one layer, alongside the forms of direct democracy that have been experienced in communitarian terms since the dawn of modernity. This image also leads us to think differently about the irruption of something new.

When, in countless struggles of the modern era, the medieval imperative mandate was reactivated as a democratic tool, this reactivation not only produced a new democratic configuration in the present but also generated space for a possible different mapping of the past, one in which the Middle Ages is open to different outcomes. It is in itself an arsenal of possibilities, and the "anachronistic" imperative mandate is a concrete possibility filled with future. This possibility emerged numerous times. It surfaced in the Paris Commune and in the 1919 Bavarian revolution. It intersects with the institution of *mandar obedeciendo* (rule by obeying) that the Zapatistas took up from the indigenous tradition.[53] In this way, to use Kantian language, the transcendental that gives unity and coherence to the historical material is external to the subject. It takes place in the energy of a historical event, which, in combining different temporalities, also shows bridges between geographically distant traditions. A different way of working with concepts can emerge. Instead of having umbrella concepts that order and subsume different particular cases, it is possible to operate with a network of bridges between different temporal and spatial dimensions. Events from the past or from different geographical and cultural contexts can be understood as incomplete experiments in justice, freedom, and equality. No experiment has the right to exclude others or to present itself as more advanced. Every single experiment is partial by nature, not only in relation to other contemporary experiments but also in relation to past experiments, which may contain a higher degree of actuality or even future than that expressed by the historical present. A solidarity with present and past generations emerges.

* * *

Revolution and Restoration extracts normativity from practices understood as theory in action. It is a kind of exemplary or epistemic normativity that emerges in social and political practices. These constitute the living archive of an alternative path to the exhausted one of today's political and critical theory. The idea is simple. Theory that uses abstract and universal categories has been under attack for decades. The use of all-encompassing, universal categories has been criticized as colonial or Eurocentric. But the alternative has rebounded, so to speak, to the opposite pole: Universal categories have been replaced by a plurality of incommensurable ontologies. *Revolution and Restoration* offers a different way of working, avoiding both the Scylla of subsuming historical material into abstract universal categories and pre-existing concepts and the Charybdis of fragmentation into incommensurable ontological islands. The universal, as I began discussing in *Insurgent Universality*, takes place at a practical-epistemic level and should be understood in terms of bridges and connections between different political experiments. It emerges in the incompleteness of each individual experiment and thus in the need to be integrated with other experiments.

In other words, universality is an incomplete and expansive network of connections not only between different places but also between different times. The development of this network is not anticipated by theory. It is a practical task and a political possibility.

The two terms in *Revolution and Restoration* form a tension from which the terms themselves are reconfigured. The modern concept of revolution was modeled on the French Revolution. In this context, a party or a faction becomes a totality. The state seeks to shape society by freeing it from archaic institutions and legal anachronisms; at the same time, revolution from above is in opposition to the restoration of the social fabric from below. The latter, as articulated in the dispersion of sovereignty into local assemblies and authorities, is stigmatized as a form of regressive democratic excess that contrasts with the progressive representative democracy of the modern state.[54] It is time to emancipate ourselves from the revolutionary "script" and normativity that arose with the French Revolution and its constitutional forms.

The "and" between revolution and restoration does not simply juxtapose the two terms; it places them in dynamic tension. The restorative dimension, when positioned against revolution, adopts its own logic—similar to De Maistre's concept of counterrevolution, where opposing revolution ends up replicating its outcome in terms of dictatorial centralization of power. However, the restoration of social institutions and obligations opens up an alternative field of possibilities that challenges state legality, individualism, and the atomistic fragmentation of society. In this sense, the restorative dimension lends substance to a revolutionary change from below, one that reactivates an anachronistic past to make way for the newest.

In the first part of this book, I present the categories that underlie the project of *Revolution and Restoration*. In the first chapter, I investigate terms such as "history" and "anachronism," "revolution" and "restoration," and "property" and "common possession." "Restoration" and "anachronism" are often construed as negative; restoration is often used as the opposite of revolution, and anachronism is something to be eliminated, both in historiography and in political practice. In the term "revolution," I consider the coexistence of different semantic layers corresponding to different revolutionary discourses, so that the ancient notions of *revolutio, restoratio,* and *restitutio* are not erased by the notion of progress that leads to the modern concept of revolution but coexist as temporal stratifications that can be and have been reactivated in specific historical events. I am not interested in the conceptualization of these terms by the celebrated thinkers of the Western canon but in their use by communities and groups during specific social and political events. What I intend to show is that if revolution, private property, and the state belong to the same dominant trajectory of political modernity, then terms like "restoration," "common possession," and the "imperative mandate" offer possible alternatives to that trajectory.

The second chapter explores the concept of property in the practice of "other forms of ownership." This chapter expands the theory implied in the practice of social property by the water war insurgents in Cochabamba. Social property compels us to work on the history and categories of property in light of this practice and its potentials. The water war insurgents did not claim particular property rights to water or its nationalization as opposed to its privatization. Instead, they were operating on the basis of obligations determined by customs and traditions that define both the reciprocal relationship between users and the relationship between users and water. The actuality of a struggle, wherever it occurs across the planet, can shed light on innovative approaches to engaging with the Western canon and mapping global history. Simultaneously, traditional and nonmodern categories can help us decipher the intricate network of practices where other ways of owning are experimented with.

The third chapter examines the relationship between democracy and the democratic excess. This chapter aims to analyze the history and the recent reappearance in some populist movements of the institution of the imperative mandate. This institution has a medieval origin and, as said in the Report (2009) of the European Commission for Democracy Through Law, is "generally awkward to Western democracies." Yet the imperative mandate appears as an anachronism in numerous events throughout modernity that have challenged the principles of political representation and national unity. The imperative mandate goes back to the tradition of municipal self-government reactivated by the Communards and workers' councils in the nineteenth and twentieth centuries, and it is incompatible with the modern centralized representative state. It remerged in many recent social movements.

The last chapter presents another case of conflict between obligations and state laws. It deals with the practice of sanctuaries in which undocumented immigrants are given refuge. Sanctuaries often refer to medieval and religious traditions whose authority is asserted as autonomous from the state. In the cases I will consider in this chapter, activists refer to their own practice in terms of legal activity and, by doing so, implicitly refer to another legal discourse and to another authority: the authority to intervene in the legal field of asylum law and immigration legislation. What emerges is a parallel and alternative legal discourse to that of the state. Even in this case, activists operate on the basis of obligations to a tradition and not in simple opposition to the monopoly of the state's power to decide who has the right to remain as an immigrant within national borders. It is not so much disobedience against laws deemed unfair but obedience to another legal system and sources of authority that are incompatible with the dominant ruling system. This chapter is intended to be an investigation into the concept of citizenship, its limits, and especially its alternatives.

Property, democracy, citizenship. These concepts form the pillars of the modern political system celebrated in the Western canon. They are the pillars of a system founded on exclusion. The first concept is based on the exclusion from common access to that which is communal; the second is centered on the exclusion of the *demos* from the theater of representatives; the third is grounded in the exclusion of foreigners. *Revolution and Restoration* is not just a critique of these concepts. We already know the *pars destruens*. We know it to the point of boredom. Instead, this book works with the frequently missing *pars construens*. It is about the configuration of new concepts: Social property offers an alternative to the dichotomy of state and private ownership; the imperative mandate serves as a corrective to democratic systems; and sanctuaries provide a legal space-time for imagining different dynamics of citizenship. To conclude, it is essential to be aware that new concepts are not neologisms. They can only arise out of the energy that flows from real tensions between incompatible systems.

1

REVOLUTION AND RESTORATION

Perhaps the time has come to ask what the term "revolution" means for our present day. And, conversely, what our present day means from the point of view of social and political change. Victor Hugo wrote that "in this century, revolution should be everywhere."[1] Today it could be said that the semantics of revolution have expanded to the point of evaporation. In 2000, the book *Révolutions*—a journey through images of the great revolutions of the nineteenth and twentieth centuries—was published. It ended with the January 1994 revolt by the insurgents in the Mexican city of San Cristóbal de Las Casas: the "Zapatista movement."[2] *Révolutions* was translated into English and published in 2020. The editor added a postscript in which he wrote that since the Zapatista uprising, "no revolution similar to the past 150 years has taken place, but there have been several *popular* movements with a truly democratic revolutionary dimension. . . . During the two decades after 2000 there were also many *popular* uprisings in Latin America"; however, "Europe and the United States did not witness revolutionary movements, but very impressive *popular* mobilizations." When the book was going to print, the editor added that "an extraordinary semi-insurrectionist upsurge has broken out throughout the United States, against police violence, racism, and social justice."[3] What can be noted, in the last pages of *Revolutions*, is that the term "revolution" gives way to other words: "insurgency," "insurrection," "upsurge," "movements," "mobilizations." The language of classes and class struggles gives way to the language of *popular* uprisings and mobilizations.

In the Zapatista documents, the adjective "revolutionary" (revolutionary laws, revolutionary forces, revolutionary government) appears more often than the noun "revolution." When the Zapatistas use the term "revolution," they also specify that it "will not end in a new class, faction of a class, or group in power."[4] The terms "revolution" and "revolutionary" integrate with another temporal dimension: that which restores history, order, legality, and respect. I want to emphasize the proximity of the terms "revolution" and "restoration." It is a temporal dimension that does not aim to hand over power from one group to another but instead has to do with a political practice that builds a social, legal, and economic present that is different in the dimension of the now. If revolution with a capital R, whose concept and praxis were forged on the model of the French Revolution, can be seen today almost nowhere, our present witnesses more humble insurgencies, whose temporality is the now-here. These are multiple political experiments with law, property, political participation, and citizenship that do not seek their legitimacy in a future to be realized but refer to the authority of legal systems and traditions that, in the building process of the modern nation statehood, have been marginalized or almost entirely destroyed. This destruction is the work of colonialism, both within and outside Europe. Often the revolutions of the twentieth century accelerated this process by imposing a forced modernization and legal synchronization of a country based on Western models. In the effort to catch up with European countries, self-styled revolutionary and socialist governments have often imposed an accelerated course of capitalist accumulation on their countries as well.

Today it should be clear that these revolutionary experiments did not represent a real alternative to the state, the capitalist mode of production, and dominant property relationships. This is why the need for alternatives is sought elsewhere. And this is where the restorative temporal dimension reemerges. This is not something entirely new. The restorative dimension has constituted a specific temporality of social and political change in every political and social transformation. Except that it was overshadowed or repressed when the revolution became synonymous with progress, moving forward or accelerating toward a future to be conquered. From the point of view of revolutionary temporality oriented toward the future and guided by the state or a party that makes itself a state, restorative temporality is channeled into a binary structure and qualified as contrary to revolution. It is important to define this binary in temporal terms because the state, or even the state discourse shared in many liberal practices, shapes society by synchronizing local legal systems defined as "archaic," shattering community authorities defined as "anachronistic," and depoliticizing the social through a new grammar of individual rights and property relations. Instead, the restorative temporality of the social allows those alternative forms, often enclosed in customs and traditions, to emerge not in simple opposition to the state but as an alternative to it.

It is the French Revolution that shows this in all clarity and constitutionalizes the work of state synchronization, both in practice and in theory. If Hegel could define the Terror, albeit "frightening," as "necessary and just" domination because it consolidated the cardinal principles of the modern sovereign state,[5] subsequently the European bourgeoisie tried in every way to get rid of this legacy. But it did not get rid of the Terror, which was incorporated into the state, its repressive apparatuses, preventive detentions, martial law, and the state of exception. Hegel presented the Terror as the dominion of abstract principles, and in the name of these principles, particularity and concrete articulations of the social were sacrificed. In this way, his philosophy, as part of the dominant canon, contributed in theory to the war against the alternative revolutionary trajectories opened up by the poor, women, and the enslaved. Once the Jacobins had done the dirty work of destroying the workers' corporations for being too reminiscent of the medieval guilds, destroying the societies of women and the *enragés*, blocking the dangerous imperative mandate practiced in the assemblies of the sans-culottes, and leveling the forms of self-government of peasant communities, then the European bourgeoisie erected its new self-image on the rubble produced by this state violence. The era of the glorification of the Declaration of 1789 and the constitutionalism of the Girondins began. It matters little that in 1802 the dominant trajectory of the modern state saw the reintroduction of slavery, which had been abolished during the Revolution, and waited until 1944 to extend the right to vote to women. The legacy of the Terror—written off because it was no longer necessary and redefined in terms of a disgraceful protototalitarian *dérapage*—was embraced by a part of the socialist movement that classified the French Revolution as a victory for the bourgeois state and held it up as a model for the revolution and the proletarian state. In this way, the model of revolution, as a way of building the nation-state and reshaping society, replicated itself countless times during the nineteenth and twentieth centuries. The alternative to the path of modern revolution does not have to be invented out of thin air. The alternative trajectory existed within the French Revolution, in the 1848 revolution, in the 1871 Paris Commune, but also elsewhere.[6]

More recently, tensions between incompatible trajectories have emerged in relation to legal and property structures. This is the case of Zapatista women who challenge the dominant Mexican law on the grounds that it "requires personalizing rights (*personalizar el derecho*), individualizing property and land tenure (*individualizar la propiedad o posesión*)," and, in the name of juridical emancipation, destroys common forms of possession and deliberation.[7] Something similar is happening in rural and semiurban Morocco. Here, too, rural women's resistance against neoliberal privatization has led to a differentiation between universal feminism and local customary understandings of morality, gender, and land.[8] What emerges is a challenge to official narratives of development and universalist human rights, on the one hand, and the emergence of alternative practices of land ownership, on the other.

From the perspective of modern law, rural, local, and indigenous institutions are out of place and asynchronous to the legal discourse of the state. However, from the perceptive of their incompatibility, a different kind of emancipation can be achieved not through formal equality recognized by the state but in collective social and political practices that are articulated within different legal grammars. These conflicts between legal systems are not reducible to the opposition between unity and plurality. The key lies in the incompatibility between legal and political systems.

* * *

The term "revolution" did not evolve along historical linear time from the ancient idea of *revolutio*, which recalls a circular time, to the modern concept of a revolution oriented toward the future and bearing an entirely new order. The modern concept of revolution as a future-oriented process, ushering in the birth of a new world, is often defined as the product of the Enlightenment and the French Revolution. However, it should be said that it is not the revolution itself that produces this image but the conceptualization of the Revolution.

I take up an observation from Koselleck's last works: "Every concept . . . has many temporal layers."[9] Temporal dimensions, instead of being represented only diachronically as successive stages on the historical timeline, overlap as historical strata. It is about working with concepts in a different way. Stop considering their evolution on the timeline, as if there were a slow inexorable progress that from the *polis* passes through the *respublica* and ends in the state. Instead, it is a question of considering these concepts as temporally stratified, so that different semantic layers coexist and, in particular historical situations produced by intense social conflicts, can also change order, making it possible for a layer that has remained underground for a long time to emerge. This is what happens with the term revolution (*revolutio*) when the restorative dimension (*restauratio*) gets the upper hand.

Originally, the terms "revolution" and "restoration" overlapped. In the English Revolution, the reestablishment of the monarchy with the return of Charles II in 1660 was designated with the term "happy restauracion" and as the completion of the revolution.[10] Indeed, Hobbes saw in the English Revolution, from King Charles I, to Cromwell, to the return to the throne of King Charles II, a "circular motion."[11] The restoration of the monarchy closes and completes the revolutionary cycle, at least until 1688, when the "Glorious Revolution" disentangled the revolution from civil war and a further semantic leap was made.[12] The term "restoration" was also used to designate the restoration of the Bourbon monarchy in France in 1814, following the fall of Napoleon, but by now it implies a clear opposition to the revolution, past, present, and to come.

However, another deeper semantic layer of the term "restoration" also emerges. And this is my second consideration. The term "restoration" appears during the English Revolution not only in the sense attributed to it by Hobbes but also with the Diggers, as an interruption of a specific trajectory of political modernity and the restoration of forms of common land ownership and self-government. This restorative dimension reemerges in numerous revolutionary processes. One could say that if the revolution becomes a project of social reorganization led by the state or by a constituent power that aims to become the state, the restoration is a defense of society, its institutions, its traditions and customs, from the state. And not just a defense but also an expression of a different political orientation of the revolutionary trajectory. Its temporality implies the continuity of tradition, the reactivation of institutions from the past and their experimentation in everyday life. This temporality constituted the social and political practice of the sans-culottes during the French Revolution. Their practice consisted of a creative connection between revolution and restoration, innovation and tradition. If, for the Jacobins, that relationship was a nexus to be broken, for the sans-culottes it was an open field of political practices. It is from this perspective that it is possible to disarticulate the revolution/restoration binary.

* * *

The circular image of the *re-volutio* is of astronomical origin. With the publication of Copernicus's *De revolutionibis orbium coelestium* in 1543, the term revolution explicitly indicates the rotation of celestial bodies. Implicitly, however, Copernicus's text brings about a revolution in the traditional cosmological framework. The *revolutio* is no longer the rotation of the stars around the earth but the earth around the sun. With the heliocentric theory, Copernicus's *De revolutionibis* represented a paradigm shift so radical as to arouse the violent reaction of Martin Luther: "This fool wishes to reverse the entire science of astronomy; but sacred Scripture tells us [Joshua 10:13] that Joshua commanded the sun to stand still, and not the earth."[13] If the earth revolves around the sun and the authority of both the Bible and the church are implicitly questioned, it means that an entire system of spatial, moral, and political orientations is wavering.

When the term "revolution" migrates into political language, it is used to describe popular uprisings and turbulent social phenomena.[14] Maiolino Bisaccioni, in a text of 1652, compares revolutions (*revolutioni*) to people's commotions and "State Earthquakes (*Terremoti di Stato*)."[15] Since revolutions arise as a result of bad governing by ministers, Bisaccioni's text explicitly addresses the princes in order to avoid new earthquakes. The term is not used to describe a rotation or restoration. Bisaccioni's intent is not descriptive but rather prescriptive: He addresses the princes, providing them with examples so as to avoid popular revolts.

In Bisaccioni, who explicitly refers to Tacitus, there is a typical gesture of ancient historiography set in a different conception of time. In ancient times, the term "revolution" described a form of order valid for both the moral sciences and for politics. Dante spoke of the "daily revolution" around the Primum Mobile, which "has a very clear resemblance to Moral Philosophy,"[16] and Polybius had made known the model of ἀνακύκλωσις as a cyclic evolution of the forms of government according to a circular trend over time. The circular conception of time represented, above all, a form of order. If the number of forms of government is limited, it must also be assumed that they repeat themselves in some sequence. And if, in accordance with what Polybius describes, there is a degenerative succession that leads from a monarchy to an ochlocracy, that is, to dominion by the masses, and from this again to government by only one, then the political problem is how to intervene in this degenerative cycle. For Polybius, the Roman Republic represented the paradigm of a mixed government in which monarchy, aristocracy, and democracy were combined together in the form of the consuls, senate, and popular assemblies. From this combination there also arose the greatness of Rome. If it was not possible to interrupt the degenerative cycle, it was at least possible to point out a form of intervention that could slow down and govern that cycle.

However, the circular image of time is an inadequate, perhaps inappropriate, form to describe a notion of historical experience characterized by order and recurrence. It is not a question of thinking that the same events return as they are.[17] The ancient conception of historical time did not know the notion of progress, but this does not mean that it was naively circular and characterized by the repetition of the same events. For Herodotus, Thucydides, and Polybius it was rather a matter of writing histories to provide contemporaries, rulers and military leaders, with historical examples that showed how, in similar past circumstances, a heroic leader or a virtuous politician knew how to make the right decision.[18] Hence the meaning of Cicero's expression *historia magistra vitae*.[19] This conception of time and history, one could say, was founded on the authority of past historical *exempla*.

Machiavelli, in the sixteenth century, expressed this crisis, which is also a crisis of authority. He needed innovative categories to understand and intervene in a present that is undergoing transformation. In *Discourses on Livy*, when he comments on the Polybian succession of forms of government, he makes a crucial epistemological leap by adding that "these variations of governments arise by chance (*a caso*) among men."[20] By introducing "chance" Machiavelli breaks the chain of necessity and interprets historical events in terms of changes (*mutazioni*) and therefore of openings to innovative outcomes. The crisis during his present day was opening up to possible bifurcations: either embrace the political productivity of conflicts or contain the crisis and give stability to the present. Machiavelli takes the former road, Francesco Guicciardini the latter. Machiavelli started from the assumption that if everything vacillates, then even the moral criteria of individual and collective leanings are in crisis; Guicciardini, instead, tried to anchor the stability of the government on the wisdom, authority, and continuity of experience of the optimates. If Machiavelli tried to grasp a political possibility of openness to change, even in the possibility of being evil, Guicciardini, emphasizing a tendential goodness of the human soul, sought to give stability to the present.

But there also emerged a third possibility in Florence. During the same crisis, Girolamo Savonarola wanted to restore "usurped liberty and the communal property," which were continuously violated by governments, thereby causing the people to be "malcontent and restless."[21] This is the restorative temporality. According to Savonarola, "Florence might return to the manner of living of the first Christians and would be like a mirror of religion to all the world."[22] In Savonarola, change has its own source of authority in the past, in the religious reference to the community of the first Christians, their freedom and communal property. The temporality of the return should not be understood as a turning back along the same trajectory but rather as a diversion from the dominant trajectory by virtue of a transcendent authority: "the manner of living of the first Christians." The temporality of the return must be understood as a new beginning made possible by the combination and reactivation of different historical strata and institutional levels. When new proprietary relationships begin to take shape, and with them new forms of political power, the tension between social and temporal strata also increases. The past becomes an arsenal to reconfigure the present and direct it toward a different future.

In the crisis of early modernity, which is also a crisis of historical experience, it is possible to identify the coexistence of different responses, corresponding to different temporalizations of time. Machiavelli poses the problem of the government of political change in the absence of stable authorities: "Variations of governments arise by chance." The historical experience that constituted the fundament of the principle *historia magistra vitae* is in crisis. The present and the historical material are temporalized from both the perspective of the present's crisis and the political attempt to open new possibilities. Guicciardini seeks stability and continuity in the authority of the optimates and in their experience. The present and the historical material are temporalized from the perspective of an alleged continuity of the historical experience of optimates as guards of stability. Savonarola refers to the authority of early Christianity to give direction to the change. The present and the historical material are temporalized from the perspective of the restoration of deeper historical layers that emerge in the tension of the present. Restoration denotes the temporality of change and has its source of authority in the past, which is to be understood as deviation from the trajectory of the present: "The manner of living of the first Christians" is practiced in the time of "now." This restoration is deeply innovative. It is not an attempt to go back in history along the unilinear timeline; instead, it generates collisions and tensions among coexisting temporal strata. "Mutazioni," continuity, and restoration not only coexist as different temporalities of historical change but also operate as different temporalizations of historical time.

* * *

According to Reinhart Koselleck, the circular conception was possible because the "naturalistic metaphor of political 'revolution' lived on the assumption that historical time was itself of a uniform quality, contained within itself, and repeatable."[23] In other words, the stability of the social structure, only rarely and temporarily altered by a civil war, also guaranteed stability in the experience of time. Again, according to Koselleck, this experience would derive from "a view of social organization based on a society of orders (*Stände*)"[24] and would constitute a stable ground of reference until the French Revolution. The dissolution of the *Stände* would replace the static image of the natural order of the *societas civilis* with the dynamic and continuous transformation of a society of individuals. This requires, on the one hand, a power capable of holding individuals together and producing unity and, on the other, the direction and governance of changes. The concept of progress, as a political concept, is a substitute concept whose authority compensates for the lack of a spatial order guaranteed by social hierarchies with a temporal order guaranteed by traditions and historical direction. Progress is the arrow of the time vector and the sovereign that gives order to events.

It is in this conceptual constellation that the concept of revolution is singularized and temporalized.[25] By becoming the herald of progress, the revolution becomes a concept of legitimacy that works polemically to delegitimize as regressive any manifestation that is contrary or dissenting with respect to the dominant course of the revolution. In *Sketch for a Historical Picture of the Progress of the Human Spirit*, written in 1793 but published posthumously in 1795, Condorcet made a twofold move by dividing history into ten epochs and allocating the tenth to future progress. On the one hand, he defined progress as indefinite and open to the future. It "will never stop" because there are no limits to the "perfectibility of the human race."[26] On the other hand, previous eras allowed for a sort of mathematical interpolation, so that Condorcet could speak "of a progress that can be represented with some accuracy in figures or on a graph."[27] In this way, Condorcet tried to provide an elegant representation of the curve of progress entangled with that of the revolutionary process. The task of politics was to keep the state and society on the tracks of historical progress, whose features needed to be better theoretically qualified.

In the second section of *The Contest of the Faculties*, Kant posed a crucial question for modernity and modern history: "Is humankind continually progressing toward the better?"[28] Kant, who introduced the term "progress" (*Fortschritt*) into the German language,[29] refers to a historical event, the French Revolution, which, as it would constitute evidence of progress, would also show that progress toward a better (direction) is possible and therefore practicable. Kant wrote:

> This event does not consist for instance in important deeds or misdeeds of human beings whereby what was great is made small among human beings or what was small made great, and, as if by magic, old and splendid states disappear and in their place others arise as if from the depths of the earth. No, nothing of the sort. . . . The revolution of a spirited people that we have witnessed in our times may succeed or fail.

It may be so filled with misery and atrocities that any reasonable person, if he could hope, undertaking it a second time, to carry it out successfully, would nonetheless never decide to perform the experiment at such a cost.—Nevertheless, in the hearts of all its spectators (who themselves are not involved in the show), I assert, this revolution meets with a degree of participation in wish that borders on enthusiasm, a participation the expression of which is itself associated with danger. This participation can thus have no other cause than a moral capacity in the human race.[30]

For Kant, the revolution shows, in the singularity of the historical event, the universality of the idea of freedom. The spectators, "who themselves are not involved in the show," participate enthusiastically in this universality of the idea of freedom, in the republican principle according to which every people has the right "to give itself a civil constitution that itself regards as good."[31] Kant's goal is twofold: On the one hand, it indicates the direction of the time vector by merging the idea of freedom with the notion of "progress toward the better";[32] on the other, it seeks to tame the revolutionary excess of freedom through a slow educational process of the people and a series of reforms *"from the top down."*[33] In this way the temporality of the *revolution* could be tamed and become *evolution.*[34] The alternative between revolution and evolution generated stances in scientific debates apparently distant from the battlefield of politics. Such was the case of the controversy that took place in the geological field between the neptunist conception, according to which rocks were formed through slow crystallization in the oceans, and the vulcanist conception, which instead maintained that rocks were formed in fire. Taking part in the neptunist hypotheses and its slow temporality meant taking a stand against revolutionary earthquakes.

Politically, if the alternative between *revolution* and *evolution* concerns the speed of change, which in both cases is led by the state, the *restorative* temporality involves different social strata and reconfigures, again using the geological metaphor, the historical strata so that older strata reemerge in the present and change its physiognomy. Restoration is not the impossible return to a former era. This Romanticism is still reactionary in that it simply reacts against a disliked present by reversing the march of time, like a train returning to the previous station by taking the same route backward. To rethink this restorative dimension of revolution, I propose a change of perspective. I will not investigate the notion of revolution and its history from the point of view of the disengaged spectator but from the perspective of social strata whose practices are dissonant with respect to the dominant course of the revolution and anachronistic, or judged regressive, with respect to the normative time of progress. From this perspective there is no evolution of the concept of revolution from a circular to a linear and progressive structure. Rather, the three discourses and the three revolutionary temporalities—circular, linear, restorative—cohabit as different stratifications co-existing within the same term in the revolutionary discourses.

* * *

During the French Revolution, the unilinear and progressive temporality was confronted with the restorative temporality of institutional structures such as the imperative mandate, the limitation of ownership, and corporate forms of common deliberation. These forms were judged as residues of the Ancien Régime, regressive phenomena, "unconstitutional, derogatory to liberty and the declaration of the rights of man,"[35] and therefore had to be wiped out. That conflict reemerged in 1830, in 1848, and again in 1871 in the form of associations and trade communities alternative to competitive, proprietary individualism.[36] They inherit something from the old confraternities of the old regime that the workers configured in terms of "*compagnonnange*" and "mutual-aid societies." They are examples of anachronism, which do not represent the survival of the ancient but the restoration and reconfiguration of traditional institutions in a new conjuncture. All these examples show a tension between the state and society. Many insurgencies take place in this tension, which can also be portrayed as the tension between the synchronizing temporality of the state and the plural temporalities of society. The sans-culottes sought a different way of practicing democracy in the reactivation of the medieval institution of the imperative mandate; the peasants strengthened local forms of self-government and common ownership of land;[37] women declared the constitution null based on their exclusion and practiced a political citizenship in the daily politics of the assemblies that exceeded the legal one; the black slaves of Santo Domingo, mixing tradition and revolution, sought not only to address inequality and unevenness but also to etch out a different course than that of abstract universalism. In putting into practice anachronistic forms with respect to the dominant, state development of the Revolution, these different social and temporal strata, even when they did not converge, did not express a backward mentality.[38] Rather, they were steering the revolution, democracy, and property relations in a different direction.

Political theory has often dealt with Condorcet, Robespierre, Saint-Just, or with the influence of Rousseau and the Enlightenment on the Revolution. More rarely has it bothered to dig into historical material to extract theory from the political practices of social strata for which the revolution was an everyday experience. I am not talking about adding a page on some figure left on the sidelines of the canonical stories of the Revolution. It is not a question of adding the names of Pauline Léon or Jean Varlet to the existing canon but of thinking about the theoretical implications of a practice of political citizenship beyond the legal recognition of citizenship and the medieval imperative mandate as a form of democratic participation that questions the modern concept of political representation. This is the virtuous *dérapage* and anachronism that the Terror crushed and modern political theory marginalized. Indeed, if we consider the Revolution from the point of view of the synchronizing function of the state, the Terror was not a *dérapage* but a refinement of state policy aimed at destroying anachronisms such as the imperative mandate and the dispersion of power in the primary assemblies. The decree of October 10, 1793, put in place a strong centralizing push of national power and, at the same time, a war against the dispersed power of many assemblies and clubs and of women's activism. The New Regime had to avoid the accommodation of collective entities of any sort since, as Mirabeau posited already, "individuals are the only elements of any society whatsoever."[39]

It is the long war waged by the state against society. This tension is also characterized by the opposition between the future-oriented new concept of revolution and the restoration of anachronistic social institutions. This temporal binary operates as a temporalizing device of both the present and the historical material. On the one hand, there is the synchronizing violence of the state that establishes a unified legal system; on the other, there are communal forms characterized by common possession and local, traditional legal systems that are defined as "anachronistic" or belonging to the "past." It is on the basis of a precise mode of temporalization of historical time that certain institutions and forms of life are subsumed into the category of the past. That is why historiography is always political historiography.

* * *

In a letter to Hans Klöres dated December 18, 1918, Oswald Spengler described the days of the German Revolution as "weeks of the greatest shame that a nation has ever lived through, when everything which is called German honour and dignity, has been dragged through the mud by our outer and inner enemies. . . . I saw from close at hand some of the revolting scenes of November 7th and almost choked with horror." Spengler looks for rules to give order to a chaotic magma he is unable to dominate. He draws a parallel with other revolutionary events: "Like the French in 1793 we must go right through to the end in our misfortune."

He concludes by stating: "I see that the German revolution is following the typical course, slow abandonment of the existing order, violent disturbances, wild radicalism, turning back. What gives us hope today is the certainty that the monarchy will arise strengthened by this crisis."[40] Spengler's 1921 essay "Pessimism?" ends with this statement: "We Germans will never again produce a Goethe, but indeed a Caesar."[41] Circular temporality is functional here in prefiguring the return of a Caesaristic era. The image of Caesarism, already used by Bruno Bauer in his history of the French Revolution to highlight the complementarity between individualism and dictatorship,[42] would become a common *topos* of cultural pessimism on both the right and the left.[43]

The German Social Democrats, faithful to a unilinear conception of historical time and a gradual development of the economy, considered the communist experiment in the German revolution premature and opposed it. The Spartacist experiment began in Berlin on January 4, 1919, in conjunction with a general strike. The revolt was immediately suppressed militarily by the Social Democrat Gustav Noske with the help of the right-wing Freikorps. The experiment continued in Bavaria. On April 6, 1919, the Bavarian Soviet Republic was formally proclaimed. In the few weeks of the Soviet republic's life, the insurgents transferred the administration of the city into the hands of the factory councils, planned a reform of the educational system, facilitated the socialization of property, and began to design a system for the abolition of paper money. This German Soviet experiment was also soon stopped, when the Social Democratic President Friedrich Ebert arranged the repression of the Soviet republic, again using the Freikorps, which would pave the way for National Socialism.

For the Spartacists in Berlin, the time of revolution was "now," as it was already real, having been anticipated in the forms of workers' self-government. "During the first 15 days of January 1919, the experience of time changed in Berlin."[44] Insurgency is not an attempt to speed up time but rather to interrupt it: to build temporal bridges with what-has-been in order to free futures that have remained blocked. In Munich, a constitutional draft stated that the "revolution has already begun *returning* to the true democracy we can find in the medieval constitutions of municipalities."[45] The revolutionary temporality that emerges in these events blends the everyday with restoration. Institutions belonging to the past are reactivated in daily life as part of a living tradition. Just as it had also happened in the Paris Commune, the future is created in the now by reshaping and blending past and present together.

In the magma of the German revolution, it is possible to isolate elements of the circular, linear, and restorative conceptions of revolution. And their tension.

A circular conception as a diagnostic-prognostic strategy of the present is found in various exponents of the "conservative revolution." For instance, Spengler had spoken of the return of the Caesars, and Edgar Jung called for a restoration of the medieval corporations, the religious and organic life of the Middle Ages, to oppose the fragmented, atomistic modern life and modern forms of secular, materialistic liberalism. In a text written in 1932, Jung wrote that the "conservative revolution" represents the restoration of those elementary laws and values without which no order is possible.[46] The appropriation and disconnection of the term "revolution" from the socialist agenda carried out in Italy by Mussolini deserves a separate discussion. In the 1920s, Mussolini understood "revolution" as a polemical term against "the retrograde and destructive counter-revolution that is Leninism," against liberal degeneration, and as authentic national restoration.[47]

Apparently, the left and right, in contending for the term "revolution," also contended for the term "restoration." Apparently, because it is in the restorative temporality, even more than in that of the revolution, that incompatible conceptions and practices emerge. When, in *The United Republics of Germany and Their Constitution* (1918) Gustav Landauer wrote "Our revolution has already begun returning to the true democracy we can find in the medieval constitutions of municipalities and provinces, in Norway and in Switzerland, and especially in the meetings of the sections of the French Revolution,"[48] this return (*zurück-kehren*) to true democracy refers to the many experiments that tried to give a different direction to Western modernity but were interrupted and left unfinished. Landauer, not unlike the sans-culottes during the French Revolution and the Communards in 1871, wrote that the "imperative mandate will be crucial, not only in the fields of government and legislation but regarding all motions presented to the people by executive bodies."[49] This, in fact, characterizes the imperative mandate and the alternative tradition of insurgent universality: Sovereignty is not displaced in the unity of the people-nation but is articulated in groups and associations. The revolution of 1919 was an experiment with the pluralism of powers. And with time.

The modern concept of revolution prioritizes the state. The conquest of state power, a new constitution as an outcome of the constituent power, the historical discontinuity, and the imposition of a *novus ordo seclorum*, are the constitutive dimensions of the modern concept of revolution. In it, the state works as a powerful legal and administrative mechanism of synchronization. It is from the point of view of the state that alternative legal systems, based on customs and traditions, forms of local self-government, and common possession of the land, appear as historical residues and obstacles on the way to modernization.

It is legitimate to ask what distinguishes the temporality of the return to the true democracy of the medieval constitutions of municipalities, as expressed in the 1918 Constitutional Draft, from that of the conservative revolution. If both can be considered as a deviation from the dominant trajectory of modernity, what separates them is the notion of order. For Luxemburg and Landauer, the ancient, feudal, theo-ontological order superior to the human kingdom had rightly been destroyed by countless revolts of the oppressed. For the theorists of the conservative revolution, that order had to be restored. Luxemburg and Landauer referred to the tradition of the struggles of the oppressed, the theorists of the conservative revolution to an aristocracy of rulers. The former practiced an excess of freedom that kept the social and political order open to changes. The others sought to reestablish hierarchies within the order and the state. The former practiced politics as a way to transcend the statist order. The others saw transcendence in the order and in the state. For the partisans of conservation, the democratic excess had to be encapsulated in the heart of the state in the form of the "undemocratic element," i.e., the political-theological core of every democratic state,[50] which could be reactivated as surplus power in case of emergency. For the democratic insurgents, the excess dis-orders the existing order by anticipating a new order of institutions that society borrows and reconfigures from the gigantic arsenal of the past.

* * *

The theories of history, which arose in the nineteenth century with the pretense of foreshadowing the future by dividing human history into successive stages, have been exhausted. Not only for theoretical reasons, but especially for practical and political reasons. In the contemporary global condition, the political capacity to control the future is increasingly questionable. Koselleck explained this inability using the concept of the acceleration and crisis of historical experience. It could be added that the global condition has decentralized not only Europe but also its historical categories. Western modernity has, for a long time, operated as an epoch of epochs and historical-geographical stages. Terms such as "Middle Ages" and "Dark Ages" were invented to express a qualitative difference between the present and the past, together with geographical differentiations. The periodization of history has also allowed the temporalization of the space that underlies colonialism. The different historical stages of European history were elevated to a normative model and geographically projected onto the rest of the world. It is a model shared by both liberals like Mill, to justify colonialism and despotic rule over populations "not yet mature" enough to self-govern,[51] and by the dominant currents of social democracy, to indicate the historical-economic course to follow in order to achieve socialism.

Today, those teleological conceptions of history, practically undermined by countless anticolonial struggles, have also gone bankrupt on a theoretical level. If it is true that the modern sense of historical distance takes shape in groups of humanists between the fifteenth and sixteenth century and it is possible that the European peasants lacked that sense of historical past as late as the nineteenth century,[52] then various questions arise that deserve to be examined in depth, or at least mentioned. In the first place, it must be possible to find traces of that tension between temporal conceptions both in the early modern age and later. In other words, if we assume that a term like "historical time" is semantically layered, at least two consequences follow. The first is that the concept of historical time does not flow on the monorail of *chronos* by subsuming and sublating "previous" conceptions. These coexist in tension with the dominant conception of historical time. The second implication regarding a layered structure of the notion of historical time can almost be taken for granted. Understanding the dominant conception of unilinear and progressive time as more adequate to the understanding of history means assuming the result to be a presupposition: History would move in a progressive direction, and therefore the more recent formations and conceptions should be understood as superior to previous ones.

Today the restorative dimension reemerges in numerous revolutionary processes. One could say that if the revolution becomes a project of social reorganization led by the state or by a constituent power that aims to become the state, restoration is a defense of society, its institutions, its traditions and customs, from the state. And not just a defense, but also an expression of a different political orientation of the revolutionary trajectory. Its temporality implies the continuity of tradition, the reactivation of institutions from the past and their experimentation in everyday life. This latter temporality constituted the social and political practice of the Diggers during the English revolution, the sans-culottes during the French Revolution, the Communards in the Paris Commune, the German insurgents in the 1919 revolution. Their practice consisted in restoring social institutions through a creative connection between revolution and restoration, innovation and tradition.

From the point of view of the state and its revolutionary temporality, the reactivation of past institutions appears as an anachronism to be removed. This is what happens in the French Revolution with the imperative mandate and corporate forms of common deliberation. And this is what happens in the Russian Revolution with the peasants' commune. This is the perspective that emerges from the temporalization imposed by the state and the dominant course of the Revolution. But if the same historical material is temporalized from the perspective of primary assemblies, councils, and rural communes, institutions such as the imperative mandate become the present and future of another way of practicing democracy. In this temporalization, pieces of the Middle Ages, as reactivated in the practice of the insurgents, splash into the present and obtain new relevance.

During the English Revolution, the Diggers intended their practice as an interruption of a specific trajectory of political modernity and the restoration of forms of common land ownership and self-government. In the "Declaration to the Powers of England, and all the Powers of the World" published in 1649, the Diggers announced the task *to restore* the "Earth as a Common Store-house for all."[53] In the religious language of this declaration, the "work of Restauration" is the "Restauration of Israel" by the "People in righteousness, not owning any property; but taking the Earth to be a Common Treasury, as it was first made for all."[54] It is what Gerrard Winstanley called the coming of the second Adam. He, "the restorer . . . causes the waters of life and liberty to run plentifully in and through the Creation, making the earth one store-house, and every man and woman to live in the law of Righteousness and peace as members of one household."[55] Winstanley and the Diggers defended an alternative way to that of "Kingly Power" and ownership, and this way takes place in the restoration of the "true ancient law of God," which operates as an alternative and superior principle of authority to the state. To restore does not mean to go back—for at least two reasons. First, because Winstanley is aware of the oppressive nature of many ancient laws and customs, and, second, the temporality of restoration does not operate along the timeline. Rather, it is a reactivation and reconfiguration of traditional elements active in different historical and social strata.

When Gerrard Winstanley refers to the original freedoms of the English people before the Norman conquest in 1066, he does *not* defend an original Anglo-Saxon law against the Norman conquerors; he does *not* defend the *iurisdicitio* on the basis of Saxon freedoms prior to the conquest that survive in the Magna Carta. Winstanley and the Diggers reactivate another historical layer. The Norman Yoke is not attacked to indicate a break between Parliament and the Crown but between Parliament and the Common People. The restoration of the "primitive freedom in the earth"[56] goes back to before 1066 and the Saxon liberties. It jumps to the "Law of the *Scriptures*" that "gives you a full freedom to the Earth, and makes Mankind *free in all his Members.*"[57] From this perspective, Winstanley abandons the entire political and legal trajectory based on private property and serfdom, including the so-called best English laws and the Magna Carta, which he considers "yoaks and manicles."[58] The Diggers did not move away from history toward the more abstract level of natural rights, because the rights of nature are not abstract principles but legal structures reanimated and reconfigured in the practices of common ownership of land. The restoration of ancient peace and freedom does not mean going back to oppressive laws and customs. It means referring to a different political and legal tradition and trajectory that has a reality in the time of now, of the reappropriation of land, and the daily practice of digging.

Another consideration must be made. Restoration also concerns the single human being. At St. George's Hill, the daily practice of true freedom, the primacy of action and digging the common land, not only restores the commonality of common land but also the "second Adam Christ, the restorer," who is in each human being and "stops or dammes up the running of those stinking things of self-interest."[59] Restoration is about both external circumstances and intimate human nature. It is not about the "new man" who will arise in a new world. It is rather an inner transformation that takes shape in the everyday practice of freedom and digging. The restorative dimension intertwines present and past, internal transformation and change of external circumstances. There are hidden bridges between Müntzer's practice of the *Entwerdung* and Winstanley's "second Adam." Internal transformation is only possible in modified circumstances, just as changing these circumstances requires a different attitude of the human, a kind of anticipation in the present of what one aims to be. In other words, the democratic excess is also a practice of subjectification, in the dual sense of the modification of the subject and the production of a collective subject that does not preexist the practice but takes shape in a network of obligations and institutions. Instead of thinking about a "subject" of change, one must prioritize change as a site of production of subjectivity. But this reversal is far from simple. It requires orientation criteria. When these criteria were placed in a future to be realized, political praxis often became a means to an end, an instrument whose legitimacy derived from the end to be realized. In this logic, the higher and nobler the end, the more the praxis receives legitimation from the future, even in the case of the most brutal atrocities. It is a case of temporalization of historical time by the future. The tense employed is usually the future perfect or future anterior, which is also the time of the constituent power: An insurrection will have been legitimized by the seizing of state power, and then it will be called "revolution." The drafting of a new constitution acts retroactively on the past, turning rebels into heroes who otherwise, in the event of defeat, would have been condemned and executed as criminals.

The traditions to which I refer operate according to a different temporality. One example is *The Restorer of Society*, published in 1801 by Thomas Spence, which can be fully included in the tradition of the Diggers. Spence called for the abolition of private ownership of land and the restoration of society to its "natural" state, i.e., small bodies or parishes, local forms of self-government that granted anybody the liberty to change their residence.[60] When Spence uses the term "natural," its meaning is opposed to the naturalization of a social order. In Spence, the term refers, on the one hand, to the revolutionary tradition of natural rights, in which "Men, Women, and Children in the Parish whether Poor or Rich" equally participate.[61] On the other, it refers to an original dimension, the same one to which Winstanley alluded when he quoted the Bible and pointed to traditional natural law. It is a dimension that transcends the existing order and therefore opens it to change. Spence does not look at the parishes as remnants to resuscitate. His gaze goes further. It turns to the rights of nature to be restored, as they were restored in the concrete practice of the Diggers and other insurgents. *Ius naturale* is a battle term. According to Winstanley, the restoration of old freedoms does not mean going back to oppressive laws and customs.[62] It means referring to a different political and legal tradition, a trajectory that has a reality in the time of now, of the reappropriation of land, and the daily practice of digging through which the Diggers did not just till the land. They were excavating temporal and historical strata.

There are nonsynchronic social and temporal strata which are reemerging today in numerous social movements. Sometimes, they make their voices heard and claim religious traditions and identities. But these strata can also move in an emancipatory direction and show the possibility of a new present, starting from a new configuration of the relationship between past and present, one capable of freeing blocked futures. By digging into historical material, political theory can extract new categories for an alternative canon of modernity. What has emerged from this excavation work is a semantic layer of the term "revolution" that the progressive and unilinear concept of time had hidden. There are events in our present, from the water war in Bolivia, to the Arab Spring, to Occupy, which have little in common with the twentieth-century concept of revolution. These events require us to rethink how we understand revolution. To the extent that the temporality of everyday experimentation with forms of life in common prevails, the "revolutionary" dimension of these events is closer to the "conservation" of institutional forms already present than to the creation of something new according to a project to be carried out. Recourse to violence, when something like this happens, recalls the medieval *ius resistentiae*, as the right-duty to restore, re-appropriate, and defend an order unjustly violated.

Today, in light of the above, the concept of "revolution," still used to express innovative political, economic, cultural, and scientific changes, should be reconsidered. Our time, if it is or can become the time of the decline of the nation-state, requires thinking about social and political changes with the language used by Machiavelli when the state was yet to be born. There are "mutations" that result from the reconfiguration of different temporal layers and temporalities. These "mutations" take place in the "here and now" of a plurality of social and political experiments, in which the democratic excess emerges not as a constituent power or theory of revolution but as a set of practices that challenge the dominant temporality of the nation-state. The present, which seems to be something that cannot be transcended—almost frozen if viewed through the lenses of the great revolutionary phenomena—takes on a different physiognomy as soon as attention is paid to the plurality of experiments that, by reactivating anachronistic temporal strata, anticipate other forms of ownership, ways of practicing politics, citizenship, and obligations. It is now a question of investigating these ways not in the abstract form of new normative theories but starting from the concrete social and political practices of humble insurgents who reappropriate forms of possession and legal and political forms from alternative historical traditions. These reappropriations have their own specific temporality.

The crisis of the present is dissolving the structure of the previous world bit by bit and renders useless many of the categories and concepts used up to now to make sense of the present era. Just as for Machiavelli five hundred years ago, chance and change once again become necessary terms in the here and now of our present. The global condition allows us to show, in the very act of their production, a plurality of bridges or, to use an expression of the Zapatista Declaration of June 2021, *From the Other Europe*, "the long and hidden thread that unites different and distant geographies and links calendars near and far."[63] The "long and hidden thread" is not brought to light by any ontology. Instead, it is woven by the practice of what the Zapatista Declaration calls "the human" as an open common experiment. The new political theory that can emerge from these political practices must be cross-eyed, in the sense that if the right eye peers into the telescope, the left eye peers into the microscope. One eye looks at a detailed political event, while the other looks at the last five hundred years of global history.

2

PRIVATE AND SOCIAL PROPERTY

On November 5, 2002, Gonzalo Sánchez de Lozada, a member of the Movimento Nacionalista Revolucionario and president of Bolivia for two nonconsecutive terms, in a public address at American University, Washington, DC, referred to social movements in Bolivia, stating that "they don't believe in democracy." Sánchez de Lozada contrasted the model of "representative democracy" to the "authoritarian communalistic democracy" based on supposed assemblies of Bolivia's indigenous society.[1] Indeed, if we take "representative democracy" as a normative model by which to judge democracy, the social and political practices that emerged in Cochabamba and the forms of assembly of indigenous communities are not compatible with the state-oriented conception of democracy. In fact, they have to do with another way of practicing democracy and property relations. The state and the social practices of the assemblies of Cochabamba share the same term "democracy," but not its semantics. One could even say, by reversing Sánchez de Lozada's statement, that if the assemblies of Cochabamba practice *democracy*, then the so-called representative democracy of the modern state is not democratic. Their grammar is not only different. It is incompatible.

During the 2000 water war mobilizations in Bolivia, a factory workers' manifesto read: "We don't want private property or state property, but self-management and social property."[2] The water war that took place in Cochabamba challenged the demarcation and opened up a field of legal and social possibilities that go beyond both the modern regime of private property and the hierarchical structures of the traditional form of community in the Andes. The experience of Cochabamba has left us the term "social property" (*propiedad social*), which is not a concept or a legal form but a practice that, better than the vague term "commons," shows us another trajectory of democracy. Social property is not the result of an appropriation or expropriation of common resources, infrastructures, or means of production but the consequence of their democratic use, or what the insurgents called *autogestión*. Let's see how the conflict has unfolded.

In 2000, the water war in Cochabamba began. The insurgents picked up the term "war" used by the press, and the mobilization became the *guerra del agua*. Cochabambinos and Cochabambinas organized themselves around the Coordinadora de Defensa del Agua y de la Vida (Coalition in Defense of Water and Life). Beneath the surface of a war for access to water, another war was taking place—one between incompatible legal and economic systems. It was a war to restore the social fabric, customs and traditions, and forms of community and collective life. This other "war" has always opened, and can open, new scenarios that can put an end to the colonial, appropriative parable.

Indeed, the history preceding the water war can be traced back to the conquest of America, Spanish domination,[3] and the imposition of a new legal and political order that overlapped and largely destroyed the indigenous one. The attack on the Indian community is manifested in the 1874 *Ley de Exvinculación* (Disentailment Law), which states: "No individual or group of individuals may take the name of community or *ayllu*, nor appear for such an entity before any authority."[4] The language of the Disentailment Law shows the incompatibility between individual private property and communal forms of ownership.[5] The Disentailment Law produced a dual effect, which was actually two sides of the same coin. On the one hand, by dissolving the communal forms of possession, it recognized the absolute right of individuals to buy and sell land, thus giving rise to a fragmentation and atomization of previous forms of common possession. On the other hand, it recognized the right of the state to expropriate land for greater reasons of national necessity. In fact, the property, deprived of the local authority to which it was linked, became a right recognized and protected by state power. But in this way, it became a right dependent on the state, which also reserved the right to expropriate it.

The law of 1874 aimed not only at unchaining the land but also at "freeing" Indians from communal bonds and hierarchies and nonstate forms of authority. In other words, it presented the modern Western grammar of individual rights as a form of emancipation from communal and oppressive relics. It would be romantic to think that it is possible to undo individualization and privatization by restoring traditional Andean practices. But these were not frozen in time but have changed in the encounter and clash with colonial Spanish codes. Colonial "property form juridically subsumed *cacicazgos* under state auspices and modified precolonial political relations by eliminating forms of indigenous social control over the succession of governors."[6] These changes reached the structure of the household. If traditionally "women were eligible to exercise authority," the Spanish law "classified married women as legal minors. This meant that any legal transaction into which a woman entered had to have the prior authorization of a man, who acted as her 'tutor.'"[7] What emerges is a mixture of Andean and Spanish legal forms not only in the institutional forms present but also in the movements that opposed Spanish colonization and dominion. There is no authentic *cacicazgo*, cargo system, or *ayllu* to resurrect, because those forms have either been dissolved or reconfigured over centuries of new practices of authority, self-government, and property. These legal systems have had to confront and interact with both Spanish colonial dominion and internal colonization by the nation-state.

Casimiro Corral, ambassador from Bolivia to the United States, member of the Liberal Party, and the president of the Constituent Assembly in 1871, wrote that "the work of modern civilization is to free from encumbrance the estates of the aristocracy and the clergy which feudalism has invented."[8] This was echoed by a document written by two anonymous lawyers from La Paz: "The states that are in the vanguard of civilization and progress in this century of steam and electricity have rushed to sell off communal, vacant, and uninhabited lands and even monastic assets, transferring them from dead hands to industrious hands, both national and foreign."[9] In the name of civilization and progress, achieved through the legal violence of the state, communal land must be transferred "from *dead hands* to industrious hands," the former being those of the backward indigenous communities and the latter those of the modern capitalist, be it national or international. For the two lawyers who drafted this text, it would be the law of progress.

In the nineteenth century, a series of legislative acts tried to dismantle forms of common property and communal self-government to make room for the new regime of individual private property. The Bolivian National Revolution of 1952 and agrarian reform of 1953 took another step toward building a unitary nation-state based on individual rights and private property. The Agrarian Reform Law of 1953, through a program of land expropriation and its redistribution, laid the foundations for an individualization of property and the erosion of the *ayllu* as an authority and jurisdictional space.[10] This was the so-called progressive character of the reforms shared by leftist parties, trade unions, and NGOs that continued along the same path, trying to impose a "modernization" of the country, free from the archaic remnants of *ayllus*.[11]

The short prehistory of the recent water war can be identified in the World Bank intervention and the presidential Supreme Decree 21060 of 1985 that, in order to stop inflation, paved the road to the privatization of state-owned companies. In the 1980s, Decree 21060 introduced new structural adjustments oriented toward neoliberal economic policies and, subsequently, a series of interventions financed by the World Bank and COSUDE, a Swiss development agency, introduced measures to safeguard and implement women's rights to landed property. To the extent that the expansion of liberalizing policies during the second half of the nineteenth century constituted an attack on indigenous tenure systems, rural communities claimed the right to undivided titling, "defending their own forms of land tenure and management administered historically through their own authority systems."[12]

The neoliberal policies of the 1980s and 1990s can be read as the unstable result of the messy encounter between conflicting forces and social strata. Privatization and liberal individualization of rights represented the so-called modernizing forces; decentralization and implementation of forms of local governance responded both to the lack of the state and its withdrawal from the social; at the same time, the state was not weakened but rearticulated according to its primordial, nondemocratic sovereign functions; sovereignty was strengthened at the level of government decision-making processes and led a constant attack on social and collective rights, trade unions, and labor organizations; legal autonomy to indigenous territories was recognized as a result of pressures from indigenous and peasant organizations. New configurations of the private-state binary emerged, as can be seen in the 1994 Bolivian Law of Popular Participation and the 1996 Land Reform Law. The former implemented decentralization reforms and the improvement of local governance,[13] whereas the latter provided the legal framework within which indigenous communities could manage their forest resources within their territories. What has to be noted is that the process of decentralization proceeded together with the privatization and decapitalization of the state.[14] The 1994 law confers legal personhood (*personería jurídica*) to indigenous communities and urban collectives, thus also giving the traditional *ayllu* "the opportunity to officially register with the state as a territorial base organization. . . . Given these new political, economic, and cultural benefits, many communities that previously identified as peasant communities (in line with the 1953 agrarian laws) now opted for re-constituting themselves as *ayllus*."[15] From this unstable neoliberal mix, we arrive at Law 2029 of 1999, which inaugurates a new season of privatization. Each phase of this long war sees the combination of economic, private, state, and suprastate violence. Law 2029 combined state intervention and privatization: The state intervenes by imposing a monopoly on resources; in this way, it attacks social and legal systems of self-management of resources at the community level; the social is thus leveled, paving the way for massive privatizations, free to impose themselves in a civil society of private individuals. It is important to keep this intertwining in mind because it shows that state intervention, its monopoly, and privatizations are not terms in opposition to one another. This script has been reenacted countless times in the modern history of colonization within and outside Europe.

Law 2029 shows this intertwining of nationalization and privatization. Article 29 states: "No natural or legal person, public or private, civil association with or without profit aims, anonymous society, co-operative, municipal or of any other nature, may provide services of water supply and sanitation in concession zones, without a concession issued by the Basic Services Superintendency."[16] In this way the state imposes its monopoly on water. The irrigators, who use their infrastructures for water distribution, are granted temporary licenses. But in fact, in a short time, they risk seeing their alternative systems of water supply, regulated according to *usos y costumbres*, become illegal. The attack, as pointed out by the Coordinadora de Defensa del Agua y de la Vida, is on each autonomous use of water, on communal or associative forms of organization, peasants and indigenous people that, through mutual-aid systems, have their own water infrastructures. Under the state monopoly, not only are infrastructures snatched from the hands of communities, but the practices of self-management and water regulation become illegal. At the same time, Article 72 of Law 2029 states that users "are obliged" to connect to the company network, undermining de jure and de facto any residue of legal autonomy. A juridical model that synchronizes alternative and, from the state's point of view, anachronistic legal systems is imposed. On this new legal basis, Article 19 of Law 2029 could be implemented: "The State will promote the participation of the private sector in the water supply and sanitary sewerage services."[17] This leads to the concession contract with the Aguas del Tunari consortium, which establishes that the concession holder has the following rights and duties with an "*exclusive nature*: transport and storage, distribution and marketing of drinking water from treatment plants or water wells to the users in the concession area" (Título II). Annex 5 of the contract makes explicit the handing over of water resources from the state to the private company according to the same monopolistic logic present in Law 2029. The same Annex 5 also states that "the use of alternative sources will not be allowed." As if this were not enough, Annex 5, Numeral 1.3 establishes that if users own alternative water sources, for instance a well, the concession holder has the right to install a metering system, with the installation costs at the expense of the user.[18] The logic of privatization went so far as to prohibit "the peasants from constructing collection tanks to gather water from the rain."[19] Since rain, as such, could not be privatized, the law simply prohibited collecting it. If in Cochabamba the collection and distribution of water developed in community forms, through committees with a two-year term and in harmony with customs and traditions, then Law 2029 declared these autonomous systems *illegal*. This is how legal synchronization of the state works.

The price of water increased as much as 200 percent as Aguas del Tunari began to take control of community-owned water distribution infrastructures. But this privatization process would not have been possible without Law 2029 and without the state power to make decisions about the country's water resources. Law 2029 and its application show that the opposition is not between state (public) and private. It is a clash between a legal system of individual private rights and a system of collective and community rights. This clash takes place on legal and extralegal grounds. The insurgents defended systems of regulation and self-management of water, which from the point of view of the state are illegal but which are in fact part of a different legal order, one incompatible with that of the state. To demolish this alternative legal order, the state used both the violence of the law as well as military and police violence under the rules of a state of emergency.

Mobilizations for the right to water began in December 1999. To defend the common use of water, the Coordinadora organized a web of assemblies at the district levels.[20] The Coordinadora arose spontaneously. After an escalation that turned Cochabamba into a war zone, the Aguas del Tunari company had to leave the country. But before arriving at the removal of Aguas del Tunari, the state exhibited its violence by declaring, on April 7, 2000, a "state of siege." Social mobilization, which turned into anger when a young student was killed by machine-gun fire from a Bolivian Army captain, forced the police to communicate to the executives of the consortium that they could no longer guarantee their safety.[21]

If the water war halted the march of privatization, bringing back state public property was no longer an option. As noted by Oscar Olivera, the "nationalization, in the end, prepared the condition for the denationalization of our collective wealth. The opposite of the cataclysm privatizations and de-nationalization of transnational capitalism is neither state capitalism nor state property."[22] This *neither-nor* logic is critical. In Cochabamba the practice of social property showed a third way, alternative to the private/public binary: "Current law . . . allows no room for social property and only recognizes classical forms of ownership: public or private, each with its variants (state, municipal, cooperative, corporate, individual)."[23] The alternative of social property can be explained not starting from concepts but as theory in action in concrete social and political practices from which new concepts emerge. Social property is the *practice* of undoing the entanglement that characterizes the concurrent birth of the state and private property. It redefines property relations through democracy. And the other way around. It shows the potentialities of democracy when the obstacle of absolute private property is removed.

* * *

In a public statement on February 6, 2000, the Coordinadora made it clear that the question of water is a question of democracy: "Democracy is the sovereignty of the people and this is what we have done."[24] But here, people, sovereignty, and democracy do not coincide with the concepts that bear the same name in the dominant canon of political thought. As it stood out in the Declaration, saving water means different regulations based on local communities, customs and traditions, and different practices of democracy. What is at stake is a practice of democracy that is not based on the state and the modern concept of representation. In another of the Coordinadora's documents we read that "we are tired of the simulation of democracy whose only purpose is to make us obedient and impotent voters."[25] Undoing the "simulation of democracy" is something absolutely concrete. It is not a question of implementing democratic procedures within the existing constitutional framework. In the language of the insurgents and the Coordinadora, it is about "recovering the voice" of the people to give rise to a "correct practice of democracy."[26] The theory of this "correct practice of democracy" must be extracted from the social practices of the insurgents and from the intersection of different traditions, from the women and the unionist tradition of the miners to the *usos y costumbres* of the peasants. To the extent that the experience of Cochabamba, like many other political experiences in which women are direct protagonists,[27] shows another way of doing politics and practicing democracy that is not based on the representation or charisma of a leader, the water war mobilization began to alter not only the social and political fabric but also people's subjectivity, habits, and mentality.[28]

The practice of the insurgents during the water war teaches us that doing democracy and undoing privatization are entangled. The democracy in action of the insurgents of Cochabamba disrupted the division between the political and the social. A different democratic practice, articulated in a plurality of intermediary bodies, local assemblies, authorities, and forms of self-government, develops on the basis of different property relationships. *Social property* implies a different vision of democracy. In the words of the insurgents, in Cochabamba there took place an "extraordinary pedagogy of democratic assemblies" not based on representative democracy, according to which a leader speaks on behalf of everyone, but on the exercise of "direct democracy," where the "power of decision-making is reappropriated by social structures, which, in their practice of radical political insurgency, derogate from the delegative habit of the state power and exercise power themselves."[29] This political pedagogy began to produce a "different way of exercising and feeling political power" and gave rise to a "reconfiguration of the state and the way to practice political rights."[30]

In the fourteenth bulletin published on February 6, 2000, the Coordinadora presented an alternative system of "irrigation and water consumption based on traditional practices" as part of a different practice of democracy. The "representative democracy," which the Coordinadora defined as a "simulación de democracia," is based on the principle of people's sovereignty.[31] But this is a "people" that is not really present but becomes visible, as a whole and unity, as represented in the various organs of the state, up to the president or the monarch who, in his person, makes the simulacrum of unity visible. Four hundred years of political theory of the modern state immediately become clear to Cochabamba insurgents when they define the "plebeian politics" that emerged in the water war as "the expansive movement of a politics of presence against the exclusionary politics of representation."[32] Political representation is the representation of the invisible *unity*, of the impossible *whole* of the nation and of its fetishistic political *identity*, which become visible through representative artifice and through an exclusionary act. Political representation simulates democracy because a leader or group of delegates speaks on behalf of the nation, *re-presents* it in the sense that it makes it visible. But it is a ghost presence.

The politics of presence is completely different. It is not based on a political identity to be produced. It is based on political presence in numerous local assemblies, communities, and associations. It is based on an expansive plurality because it is open to anyone who participates politically in the life of the assemblies. In Cochabamba, unity is disarticulated in the plurality of groups that do not need to be represented, because they are present.

What the Coordinadora called a "correcto ejercicio de la democracia" is a vision of insurgent democracy as a practice. Not the crowd, the multitude, or the constituent power but a rich institutional fabric of democratic practices and local assemblies. It is a kind of "vernacularized" messy democracy.[33] It is this set of democratic practices that makes the state nervous. A riotous mass can be a challenge, quite a dangerous one, to the establishment and to what the state calls "public order." But it does not question its grammar. The state is organized violence and is familiar with the language of violence, which from time to time it unfolds through the state of emergency. The state, instead, is allergic to the democratic excess that manifests itself on a social level as a democratic practice of dispersion or vernacularization of power in numerous local assemblies. This democracy in action exceeds the representative form of the modern state, but it is not formless. Its institutional structure challenges the state monopoly on decision making and restores the collective capacity to deliberate, "to recall, to hold accountable, and to force leaders and representatives to adhere to collective decisions."[34] It is in this intertwining of political practices, local self-government, and forms of common ownership that the term "social property" takes shape. It is what Sánchez de Lozada defined as "authoritarian communalist democracy" based on supposed assemblies of Bolivia's indigenous society.[35] It is a matter of a plurality of local assemblies, the reference to customs and traditions, and to the *ayllu* as an institution and practice of "other democracy." Here, the *ayllu* must be understood as the name of an institution that challenges the process of social atomization imposed by the state.

In the water war there emerges a different legal trajectory based on customs and traditions (*usos y costumbres*) of the common use of water and infrastructures. This different trajectory, which from the state's point of view seemed in many ways illegal, was also presented in terms of a "Copernican inversion" that "involves displacing the centrality of 'state' and 'institutional power' as a privileged space for politics to instead situate it in the polyphonic and plural social capacity for insistently distorting the heteronymous political order."[36] *Usos y costumbres*, often defined as anachronistic, constituted a legal and temporal barrier to the privatization not only of water but also of society and politics. A legal barrier because they are grounded in common obligations and rights. A temporal barrier because traditions came into conflict with the "progressive" temporality of neoliberal privatizations. A barrier to the privatization of politics and society, finally, because communities and groups became protagonists of the democracy of presence through institutions articulated in a "system of reciprocal obligations."[37]

* * *

Following the theory in action of the Coordinadora, this democratic practice is articulated through diverse forms of reappropriation.[38] The verb *reapropiarnos*, to reappropriate (to ourselves), does not express a change in ownership but the undoing of private and state appropriation. It both indicates reclaiming possession of something that has been taken away and refers to a different tradition of democratic political practice, as well as a different semantic usage of the term "proper." The term "proper" here denotes a restorative movement, the act of putting things right after centuries of colonial violence. This restorative inversion of time is expressed in the term *"pachakuti,"* which expresses the idea of turning or inverting time and space, of returning to a new beginning.[39] *Pachakuti* contains the assumption that the cosmic order will be restored, in the sense of "a past capable of redeeming the future, of turning the tables."[40] This restorative dynamic must be kept in mind to understand the political grammar of rights as practiced in Cochabamba. It is not a question of a return to a museum-like past and much less one of power changing hands. *Pachakuti* has semantic layers that differ each time, depending on the circumstances. One of these, perhaps the most appropriate for understanding the present, is characterized by a particular type of inversion, i.e., from "inside to outside."[41] The alternative legal structure made up of forms of self-government, common possession, and reciprocal obligations, attacked by the dominant structure of the state, private property, and individual rights, has found refuge within a community system of local practices. *Pachakuti* can also be this: the spilling over of this system from the inside to the outside, not as a question of scale but as a change in a form of life and its legal and institutional structures. To use the language of the Cochabamba insurgents, it is a set of alternative practices of self-government that shape the "community or extended *ayllu*."[42] Or, quoting another insurgent, "a new institutional framework *(una nueva institucionalidad)*."[43] This does not appear out of nowhere but is constantly produced and reproduced in the social as a combination of past and present legal structures.

The 2000 Declaration lets us glimpse the political theory of new *institucionalidad*. It states that the polyphony of voices and actions of social mobilizations "gather together today in solidarity to combine forces in the defense of the vital right to water."[44] The vital right (*derecho vital*) inverts the logic of modern law. It is not based on the will of individual subjects and on their right to have common resources such as water. Rather, the vital right is based on the vital need to access those resources not only for individual survival but for the existence of forms of community life. The defense of the "vital right to water" goes beyond the specific object, water, and is configured as a defense of customs and traditions, forms of life, and community practices whose legal existence is based on reciprocal obligations.

In the name of the "right to life (*derecho a la vida*)," of the *usos y costumbres*, of existing local authorities, the insurgents have created a "space" for a different kind of politics, democracy, and democratic participation.[45] The grammar of the "right to life" is more in the order of duties and obligations than of rights. It implies respect for nature, customs, and the chain of generations that relate to nature or, in this concrete case, to water. In the formula "reappropriate our rights," the rights that are reappropriated are "rights" of a different nature. One could say that the term "right" is here a false cognate. Indeed, the term "right" is not the common denominator guaranteed by the state, even with social pressure from below. These are legal forms that refer to and reconfigure community systems of self-government according to the *usos y costumbres* of the Andean tradition.[46] By analogy with the Western system, one could speak of collective rights. But the comparison immediately shows limits. The forms of work-shifts and the system of reciprocal obligation, known as the system of *mitas y suyos*,[47] leads into the practice of the commons better than the concept of collective right or the common good does. The two terms, *mitas* and *suyos*, connect a spatial dimension, strips of land (*suyos* in Quechua), and a temporal dimension, relating to the performance of work-shifts and service (*mita*).[48] This space-time combination places particular emphasis on a system of shifts, working for the community, accountability, reciprocal obligations, and role rotation. Together the two terms denote an organization of the territory, the regulation of agricultural cycles, access to resources, a government of the common forms of housing in the territory. In other words, a common form of being in the world. The result is that, in this context, the terms "right" and "life," included in the right *to life*, express not a subjective right extended to the entire world of the living but an institutional form of life—a way to inhabit the space, regulate the shared use of resources, assume authority and responsibility in the government of the community.

In this legal configuration, the right to use water is not an individual or collective right guaranteed by the state. It is the common use by the users within a legal system autonomous from the state. Indeed, in this alternative juridical configuration, water is not the target of a subjective right to property. Rather, water has juridical priority. This is an inverse relationship to that of modern Western modern law. If the latter is prompted by the individual will of the subject who exercises the right to property over external things, the grammar of the right to life instead gives priority to the use and, therefore, to the *way* in which social groupings relate to a common resource, according to regulations that go beyond individual rights and are instead rooted in the *usos y costumbres*.

In the practice of social property, property relations take place at a distance from the state and are part of democratic regulations at the local level. It is the community through its own institutions that collectively discusses and decides on common and individual use and on the most appropriate way to preserve common resources. In this way, users are bound to one another by a "system of reciprocal obligations,"[49] which also involve resources used in common. These become a subject among subjects and not, as happens instead in the modern concept of private property, an object of individual will. This system is not based on an alternative ontology[50] but on different legal practices and property relations.

* * *

On April 11, 2000, the Bolivian government was forced to repeal Law 2029 and issue a new law, number 2066. It contains thirty-six articles, which, in addition to keeping open the possibility of creating a national water council, recognize traditional *usos y costumbres* and the presence within the territory of local units of popular participation.[51] Although the Coordinadora won the battle against water privatization by forcing the Aguas del Tunari company to leave the country, at that point a new level of discussion and conflict regarding the future of the municipal water supply company (SEMAPA) was opened. It must immediately be said that the Coordinadora's attempt to restructure SEMAPA on the basis of customs and traditions—on the basis of the practice of social property and social control—failed.[52] The Coordinadora tried to transform SEMAPA into a sort of social enterprise, a water management system organized on the basis of local authorities revitalized in social practices.[53] Raquel Gutiérrez-Aguilar rightly observed that "current law . . . allow[s] no room for social property and only recognizes classical forms of ownership: public or private, each with its variants (state, municipal, cooperative, corporate, individual)."[54]

Little could be done within the existing legal framework. There were at least two main obstacles on the path to real reform and social reappropriation of

SEMAPA. On the one hand, the practice of social property was incompatible with both the regime of private property and state property; on the other hand, the forms of local authority and self-government were incompatible with the notion of unitary state sovereignty. Different, incompatible legal systems were set up against each other. The water war's history and aftermath show that these systems cannot coexist side by side for long. SEMAPA returned to public hands under the control of municipal government.[55] The 2009 Bolivian constitution and the 2010 Universal Declaration of Rights of Mother Earth put an end to the social property experiment. The latter, signed in Cochabamba on April 22, 2010, is an example of political contraction through ontological extension. The declaration presents Mother Earth as a "living community of interrelated and interdependent beings with a common destiny," where the "term 'being' includes ecosystems, natural communities, species and all other natural entities which exist as part of Mother Earth."[56] This is the ontological extension. From here the declaration turns toward the usual language of human rights and speaks of the necessity "to recognize and defend the rights of Mother Earth and all beings" through "prompt and progressive measures and mechanisms, national and international."[57] Essentially, in so far as Mother Earth has "the right to be respected," all "States, and public and private institutions" have a duty to recognize and protect those rights.[58] The interdependence proclaimed at an ontological level, translated into juridical language, presupposes a national and international power that guarantees the rights of the vulnerable subject. If there is politics, in this as in other similar declarations, it is only on the part of the state and a power capable of protecting politically passive subjects.

A further step in this direction was taken in an attempt to constitutionalize claims relating to the defense of water and Mother Earth. In December 2010, Bolivia's Plurinational Legislative Assembly passed the Law of the Right of Mother Earth.[59] Here a vague reference to the cosmologies of rural indigenous people allowed the legislator to list the rights of Mother Earth and, more importantly, to affirm state obligations to guarantee and protect them (Art. 1). This integration does not add much to what is already contained in Article 34 of the 2009 Bolivian constitution: "Any person, in his own right or on behalf of a collective, is authorized to take legal action in defense of environmental rights, without prejudice to the obligation of public institutions to act on their own in the face of attacks on the environment."[60] Each intervention, be it on an individual basis or in the name of the collective, is mediated by the state in terms of legal actions. A similar grammar is also found in Ecuador's 2008 constitution, which, in Articles 71, 72, and 73, combines the indigenous language of *Pachamama* with the legal one of the state. The result is the translation of nature into a thing to which the state attributes rights that the state itself should then protect.

A kind of juridical algebra emerges. The longer the list of rights, the more extensive the power that must protect those rights. And, consequently, also the discretion of that power. In Bolivia, even though Art. 2.6. of the Law of the Right of Mother Earth proclaims that the "exercise of the rights of Mother Earth requires the recognition, recovery, respect, protection, and dialogue of the diversity of feelings, values, knowledge, skills, practices, transcendence, transformation, science, technology and standards, of all the cultures of the world who seek to live in harmony with nature," the Morales government, without prior consultation with the local populations, decided to build a 190-mile road through the Isiboro Sécure Indigenous Territory and National Park (TIPNIS).[61] Fernando Vargas, a TIPNIS indigenous leader, accused Morales of not being "a defender of Mother Earth, or indigenous peoples." He added that "this is the beginning of the destruction of protected areas in Bolivia and indigenous peoples' territory."[62] The government's decision perhaps contradicts the spirit of the declaration of the Rights of Mother Earth, but the power of the state is not limited either by the Rights of Mother Earth or by the acknowledged local autonomy of indigenous peoples. In this regard, the inadequacy of the attempt to integrate indigenous rights into the liberal democratic framework of rights and human rights should be noted. The incompatibility of the two legal trajectories concerns not only the difference between individual and community rights but also, and above all, the priority given to reciprocal obligations over subjective rights and to forms of common possession over private property.

Although Article 30 lists a long series of rights granted to "rural native indigenous peoples," all these rights depend on the state to guarantee and protect them.[63] And insofar as they depend on the state, the state can also limit and suspend them. Therefore, what Evo Morales stated on July 31, 2011, is not in contradiction with the constitution: "We are going to do consultations, but I want you to know that they are not binding. [The road] won't be stopped just because they [the Indigenous peoples] say no. Consultation is constitutionalized, but is not binding, and therefore, the great desire we have for 2014 is to see the Villa Tunari–San Ignacio de Moxos road paved."[64] It is not a question of blaming Evo Morales for his inconsistency with regard to the promises he made in the election campaign or his references to *Pachamama*. When he refers to the *bien común*, the common good of the country, he refers not only to the will of the majority, to which the minority must adapt, but also to the Bolivian people as a whole and to its unity, which he represents. His rhetoric often took the form of internal colonialism, accusing indigenous peoples of being backward, of constituting an obstacle to national development, of being manipulated by foreign powers.[65] From the standpoint of the state, "backward" is anything that is out of sync with the rhythm of the state's legal and economic system. This represents the tip of the arrow of historical time, and everything that is not appropriate to its time is de facto and de jure backward. Tensions between temporalities and between unity and plurality can only be resolved within the legal framework of state sovereignty, i.e., on the side of unity. And by the president who represents it. His power ranges from declaring a state of emergency in "the case of danger to the security of the State" (Art. 137) to the normal use of presidential decrees, such as that used in October 2010 by the Morales administration to open up fifty-six new areas for oil development, some of which were on indigenous territories and other protected areas.[66]

As also reiterated by the vice president of Bolivia, Álvaro García Linera: "Besides the people's right to land, the State—the State led by the indigenous-popular and peasant movement—has the right to prioritize the higher collective interest of all the peoples. And this is how we proceeded afterwards."[67] Linera's language, like Morales's, is the language of the modern representative state. When he writes that the "Amazon is ours, it belongs to Bolivians," the subject is "OUR State, our legislation, our government and our state public policies."[68] Morales and Garcia Linera talk about the state's power to make decisions, including the decision on the state of emergency and the suspension of some fundamental rights. What merges in this and other similar examples[69] is the clash between incompatible legal-political trajectories. Evo Morales and García Linera acted in the name of progress and superior national interest, which also includes indigenous peoples who opposed the construction of the road. Paraphrasing Rousseau, it could be said that within the framework of the modern concept of sovereignty, the particular will of the indigenous peoples has only one possibility, which is to conform to the general will of the state. If they refuse to obey, they will be "forced to be free"[70]—in the name of progress and superior national interest.

The tension between unity and plurality is implicitly contained in the definition of Bolivia as a "Unitary Social State of Pluri-National Communitarian Law (*Estado Unitario Social de Derecho Plurinacional Comunitario*)." Article 2 does not hide the tension when it states that "indigenous peoples and their ancestral control of their territories, their free determination, consisting of the right to autonomy, self-government, their culture, recognition of their institutions, and the consolidation of their territorial entities, is guaranteed within the framework of the unity of the State, in accordance with this Constitution and the law." Plurality is recognized, but within the framework of the unity of the state and within the limits established by the constitution. Recognition means dependence on the state grammar of modern law.

Predictably, this tension extends through the various articles of the constitution. Articles 190 and 290 refer to indigenous autonomy, authorities, and jurisdictional functions, even including (Art. 290) the expression of their will through consultation, but always in accordance and harmony "with the Constitution and the law." This is the feeble voice of plurality. But in the constitution the baritone voice of the state is dominant. Article 378.I. concerns the different forms of energy and strategic resources that are essential for the development of the country; the second paragraph clarifies that it is "the exclusive authority of the State to develop the chain of energy production in the phases of generation, transport, and distribution." Article 298.II leaves no doubt that the "central level of the State has exclusive authority" over natural resources, minerals, and water sources.[71] Article 349.I reiterates that "natural resources are the property and direct domain, indivisible and without limitation, of the Bolivian people, and their administration corresponds to the State on behalf of the collective interest." The Bolivian people, as a whole and unity, only exists through the state that represents the nation, which therefore has "direct domain" on natural resources. Indeed, if according to Article 356, "the activities of exploration, exploitation refining, industrialization, transport and sale of nonrenewable natural resources shall have the character of state necessity and public utility," then from the previous articles it follows that this character of necessity and public utility is decided by the state.

In 2004 the Bolivian Constitutional Court refused to recognize an "indigenous claim to communal property on the grounds that it violated the right of private property, ruling that 'customary law . . . is not applicable to resolve a possible conflict of the right of property over land.'"[72] The language of the Indigenous and Tribal Peoples Convention Article 14 of ILO Convention No. 169 (Indigenous and Tribal Peoples Convention, 1989) shows the problem well. The first paragraph of Article 14 speaks of recognition of the "rights of ownership and possession of the peoples concerned over the lands." But the second paragraph clarifies the meaning of that recognition and the dependence of the property on the government that shall "guarantee effective protection of their rights of ownership and possession." Finally, the third paragraph clarifies that the entire dynamics of property relationships takes place within the state legal system: "Adequate procedures shall be established within the national legal system to resolve land claims by the peoples concerned."[73]

Today, not only has private property become an unquestionable dogma, but its constitutive categories have been naturalized to the point that, even when trying to think of an alternative, it operates according to modern property grammar. The legal language of the Bolivian constitution remains a simulacrum of democracy, leaving no room for the practice of social property and neutralizing the democratic excesses of local assemblies and authorities.

TO HOLD LAND DIFFERENTLY: ANOTHER WAY OF OWNING

What does it mean to engage with the concept of social property as it emerges from the practices of the water war? How do we extract theory from practice and recognize the latter as a new form of theory in action?

The water war opened up a "space" of practical and theoretical experimentation that allows for the construction of temporal and geographical bridges with legal structures and forms of ownership alternative to modern Western ones. This "space" has been hidden by the dominant juridical forms, but it characterizes and has characterized human life in an incomparably more extensive way than the brief parenthesis of Western European property relations can represent. Western modern law, in its celebration of formal freedom and equality, is not only despotic when exported to the rest of the world;[74] it is also despotic toward temporal, legal, and social strata within Europe. This is the colonial war being fought inside and outside Europe. If these two sides are not kept together, the project of decolonization will inevitably get stuck halfway through.

The notion of social property that emerges in the practices of the water war insurgents allows for a reconsideration of past practices, such as those for the defense of the commons, and the legal theory of common ownership all the way back to the European Middle Ages and beyond. And vice versa. Reexamining these legal archives allows us to return to the present with different eyes and to expand the notion of social property as a category for a new canon of politics that emerges in the tension between incompatible legal trajectories.

In the concept of private property, prejudices and ideologies of all kinds are condensed. An example is the story of the tragedy of the commons, according to which the behavior of "each herdsman," who "seeks to maximize his gain" and to put in the commons as many sheep as possible, has been defined as "rational."[75] From this point of view, in the absence of private property, a "rational being" would see no point in refraining from adding more sheep, to the point of ruining the pasture. Underlying the assumption of the tragedy are two fundamental errors: The first is to assume that the commons are not social structures regulated by obligations, community institutions of self-government, traditions, and customs. In other words, the complete lack of the sense of the past. The principle of co-obligation is contained in the same etymology as the term commons: *cum-munus*, where the prefix means "with" and *munus* expresses service, duties, and obligations. The practice of the commons suspends the full right to dispose of and alienate property, because users relate to common resources as usufructuaries who take care of them. The commoners, even if they decided unanimously, could not claim the right to destroy the resources available to recklessly extract raw materials and exploit the land to be cultivated. To do so, they would have to violate their obligations toward customs and traditions and therefore toward generations past and those to come. Therefore, they would cease to be commoners.

The second error consists in the projection of possessive individualism onto a metahistorical form. Both errors are the expression of a theory that eliminates historical depth to provide a flat and universal image of the present. It is ideology in the worst sense of the term. This chapter aims to dismantle this ideology from the perspective of alternative proprietary practices and trajectories to that of the dominant modernity. To do this, a different theoretical and historiographical working method is needed. It is not a question of contrasting the tragedy of the commons with the equally ideological comedy of a happy ending. In place of this, it is a question of working with the compresence of and tension between different historical-temporal strata. From this perspective, the story of the tragedy of the commons confirms that what has been defined as "rational," i.e., the rapacious behaviors of possessive individuals, is a weapon in a historical struggle that took form by defining as "irrational" the behaviors of the commoners, to which it is counterposed.

Rethinking the commons does not mean adopting an anthropological, community assumption instead of an individualistic, possessive one. Even if it were accepted that individuals aim to maximize their gain to the point of ruining common land, the commons are generally characterized by mechanisms of rotation and distribution of the lands, which ensure that the land is taken care of, not out of goodness but for the simple reason that devastating a plot of land—besides being irrational because devastated land could also doom the devastator—is prevented by common forms of regulation and punishment. The analysis of concrete historical forms of common possession shows that the superiority of private ownership over other property regimes is a modern myth; that the violent introduction of individual land titles from above, without considering preexisting customary rights, has created devastation and regression; that the link between private property and productivity is false; and that communal land tenure is not an obstacle to development.[76]

My focus is mainly on the structuring of modern private property relations from the perspective of multiple past and present alternatives. The concept of social property shows us the emergence from the social of legal structures that combine democracy and alternative proprietary relations. From the point of view of the dominant trajectory of Western modernity, these alternatives survive in the present as anachronisms. But what these anachronisms show is the compresence of different temporal layers in tension with one another. Alternatives to the dominant conception of private property can be found in non-Western legal experiences and in deeper layers of Western history. However, non-Western and ancient legal structures do not offer ready-made solutions. We must resist the temptation to subsume different forms of possession into the convenient umbrella concept of "commons."[77] Provisionally, it is better to stick with a more comprehensive term, such as the one used by Carlo Cattaneo to describe legal forms of common possession in the Alps on the border between Italy and Switzerland in the mid-nineteenth century: "These are not abuses, they are not privileges, they are not usurpations; it is *another way of owning*, another legislation, another social order, which, unnoticed, has descended from very remote centuries to us. Throughout the region adjacent to the Alps, the dominion of two laws, two societies, two different and opposite principles endures simultaneously."[78] At the end of the nineteenth century in northeastern Italy, municipal woods were regarded by the population as common property. While taking fruit or wood was considered theft under the new legal system of the kingdom, it was not seen as such in the common conscience of the local people.[79] The attack against these forms of possession lasted for centuries. On Italian soil, it took the legal intervention of the Fascist regime, in 1927, to shatter forms of common rights and possession.[80]

* * *

In Russia, in 1917, in one of the numerous protocols of the peasant villages, one could read that "land belongs to the peasant commune (*mir*), to the working community. This land cannot be sold, cannot be an object of buying and selling . . . land cannot belong to anyone."[81] The sacred and therefore nonappropriable character of these resources was very much present in Russian peasant awareness: "The land we share is our mother . . . selling land created by the Heavenly Creator is a barbaric absurdity. The principal error here lies in the crude and monstrous assertion that the land . . . could be anyone's private property. This is just as much of violence as slavery."[82]

Another population that feels the same way about land are the 'Are'are of Malaita in the Solomon Islands. In their view, land is "not simply soil, but rather an entity always fused with the ancestors, under whose joint authority the living are placed."[83] In this context, we understand the constant opposition of the 'Are'are people to the colonial attempt to introduce private property relations over land. In the 1980s, in a document drawn up by Erehau, leader of the Maasina Ruru movement, we read: "'Are'are people do not own the land. The land owns 'Are'are people. The Land owns men and women; they are there to take care of the land."[84]

Another example. In Andean culture, the land is not thought to be a natural resource at the service of indigenous people but as their Mother Earth (*Pachamama*), "which is why they give their lives to defend her."[85] The profound relationship they have with land, plants, and animals "makes their suffering when nature is destroyed all the greater."[86] Water and land constitute a single entity that cannot be appropriated, because, to use Western categories, it is not an object that stands before a subject. Even if in an improper way, it could be said that it is another subject with whom one relates. In the indigenous Andean culture, the term used to characterize this nexus of reciprocal relations is *ayni*, which implies a dialogue and reciprocal bond. In the rural areas of Cochabamba, the attempt to privatize and commercialize water violates all customs and traditional norms. As a Cochabamba woman put it, "If God gave us water, no human being should take it away."[87]

One more example. In the language of Dogrib, a group of indigenous people inhabiting the territory of present-day Canada, "land" is understood in relational terms that include not only land but also people, animals, trees, rivers, and lakes. From this perspective, "within this system of relations human beings are not the only constituent believed to embody spirit or agency. Ethically, this meant that humans held certain obligations to the land, animals, plants, and lakes in much the same way that we hold obligations to other people. And if these obligations were met, then the land, animals, plants, and lakes would reciprocate and meet their obligations to humans, thus ensuring the survival and well-being of all over time."[88]

The Maori leader Hone Heke had a clear idea of this when he wrote to the governor: "We do not understand your thinking and you do not understand ours. God has given this land to us. It cannot be cut into strips like whale blubber."[89] Incompatibility breeds misunderstanding on both sides. While indigenous conceptions of land cannot be judged as premodern, they cannot simply be borrowed as alternatives to dominant forms of ownership. We have to dig into the different forms of ownership and, while we are digging, invent the tools for digging.

The Incan peasant, the 'Are'are people, and the Dogrib do not share ontology or cosmological vision, but they do share property structures *not* founded on private or national ownership of the land. They could probably subscribe to the affirmation of the Russian Christian peasants when they say that making land private property "is just as much of violence as slavery." The meaning of this equivalence of private property with slavery does not lie in the commercialization of something (or someone) living. The Russian peasant did not think in terms of commodification. Private property is rather the suppression of the relational fabric constituted by reciprocity and mutual obligations. The relational vision can also be studied in the European Middle Ages. Its juridical conception was extraneous to the concept of private property and placed at its center not individuals with their rights but the thing, the *res*, with the multiple relations of use and limitations connected to it. This conception and practice of ownership has been defined as *rei-centric*,[90] thus differentiating it from the modern Western practice characterized by the primacy of the sovereign subject over things. The *rei-centric* conception gives priority to the collective fabric that embraces individuals and groups. In a world where everything, or much of it, was considered sacred, property was not sacralized. It was not an expression of the sovereign will of the individual. Rather, it was divided into various legal dimensions, such as the *dominium directum et utile*, of a complex reality.

The medieval notion of *dominium utile* carries within it an alternative vision of property, a glimpse of the past that can shed light on present struggles. This notion contained a nonanthropocentric and nonindividualistic anthropology that, first of all, made reference to a shared property, according to the different degrees of utility and use.[91] Second, the reference to *utilitas* meant a limit and a content to the property relation, which could not be understood in the abstract. Medieval conceptions are articulated in terms of use, of relations of use with respect to what is common, and of relations between users. In other words, if God is the owner, we are usufructuaries.[92] Hence the centrality of reciprocal obligations and limitations. The duty to take care of what is common, namely, land, water, and resources, rather than the right to appropriate them. It could be said that the medieval notion of property could be understood as a system characterized by upward and downward reciprocal obligations, where priority is not given to the individual but to the complex of relationships between individuals and the thing.[93]

The modern Western proprietary subject is characterized by an expansive tendency of dominion of the self, its body, and the external world. Hegel was right to derive the modern concept of private property from the concept of the person as infinite free will.[94] According to Hegel, the person, inasmuch as he "has the right to place his will in any thing," removes from that thing its exteriority by imposing on it his will, his ends, and his soul.[95] And so follows "the absolute *right of appropriation* that which human beings have over all things,"[96] a right that makes the human being the "lord over all of nature."[97] There are no obstacles that the infinite free will is unable to break down, and there are no territories that are precluded from its right of appropriation. Both one's own body and external nature must take on the form that free will imposes upon them. It is this perspective of abstract right and freedom that Hegel expounds as the presupposition of the modern era. Hegel defined it as "abstract" because it lacks the concreteness of relations, duties, and limitations that characterize the ethical sphere. It follows that it is not possible to question the modern concept of private property and the absolute right of appropriation without questioning their logical foundations, i.e., modern individual rights and individual freedom.

In the Middle Ages, individuals perceived themselves as part of a larger cosmic order, which can be represented as a world of limitations and mutual obligations. This conception does not express a particular ontological view but a world of different property relations characterized by a rei-centric legal system in which land is *not* an object of ownership and individuals are *not* sovereign subjects free to dispose of it as they please. If we pay attention to the affinity between the Andean peasant, the Russian peasant, and the medieval conception of respect for land and water, it is evident that it is not just a question of differentiating between ontological conceptions based on a matrix of relations rather than on the sovereign subject. Those forms of life are based on specific property relationships and legal and political practices.

* * *

The comparison between communal forms of ownership and private property had provoked Henry Maine's interest in Indian village communities, Ludwig Maurer's interest in the German *Marke*, and August Haxthausen's interest in the Russian *mir*, as well as Fustel de Coulanges's dispute with "primitive communism." The simplest way to explain possible analogies lies in the negative character of the similarities constructed from the contrast with the modern Western concept of property. This contrast shows us that the modern concept of private property, far from being absolute and eternal, represents only a very narrow

geographical-historical episode of human history. If this episode is not considered according to some historical teleology, it is not even at the apex of some
progress of legal forms. Common forms of ownership and common rights cannot be treated as a remnant of barbarism to be civilized, or just, as Thomas Paine
stated in 1792, "too absurd to make any part of a rational argument."[98] Nor can
they be evaluated according to the criteria of capitalist efficiency, understood
as production for the market. Rather, they are a plurality of experiments in law
and ownership, of which modern private property is only a very small part. Its
uniqueness lies in its having presented itself as absolute and as an expression of
the most advanced point of civilization. Today, in the light of numerous conflicts
that reactivate different legal traditions, and also in the light of environmental
disasters caused by the unlimited exploitation of nature, the modern conception
of private property and its legal and ideological assumptions are being questioned. It is again possible to learn from other legal experiments with ownership.
New forms emerge from social tensions and concrete struggles. New concepts
are produced in these clashes that make it possible to draw new connections
between different forms of ownership. From this perspective, I reconsider the
European Middle Ages as an archive of possibilities. And it is in this direction that
my excavation of medieval categories of ownership moves.

The point of view of the European Middle Ages can be represented by what
can be read in *Summa Parisiensis* (1160): "By divine right everything is common
(*jure divino omnia esse communia*). In fact, in goods we are usufructuaries of
the world and only God the owner, precisely because natural things are common, such as land, water and such things over which someone has usufruct by
natural law, but not ownership."[99] This is a legal tradition rooted in natural law.
It is found in Thomas Aquinas: "In the case of need everything is for common
[use] (*in necessitate sunt omnia communia*). Subsequently, it is not a sin to
take another's property, [because] need has made it common property. . . . If
the need is so manifest and urgent as to require immediate relief with the things
one has at hand [for example, when a person is in some imminent danger that
cannot be resolved in any other way], then it is lawful for a man to succor his
own need by means of taking, either openly or secretly, another's property. This
naturally is not theft or robbery (*furti vel rapinae*)."[100] According to natural law
(*ius naturale*), one who "has in overabundance is meant for the service of the
poor" and has precise obligations to provide for the needs of humankind.[101]
These obligations arise from the natural order established by Divine Providence.
From this order conforming to *reason*, it follows that, in the event that the need
is "manifest and urgent," it is permissible for the poor man to take "either openly

or secretly another's property." And this, properly speaking, concludes Thomas Aquinas, "is not theft or robbery."

This conception presents itself as very distant from the modern Western conception of private property.[102] To shed some light on this alternative repertoire of legal categories relating to property, it may be helpful to delve deeper into medieval juridical material. In the twelfth century, the Italian canon lawyer Huguccio of Pisa had already clearly expressed the problem. In the *Summa Decretum* he wrote that "those who in case of necessity (*per necessitatem*) [appropriate something of another person] they do not commit theft, because they believe or could believe that the owner would have given his permission."[103] Huguccio found an elegant solution capable of reconciling different legal systems. On the one hand, according to natural law, things are communal (*iure naturale omnia sunt communia*); on the other, the Corpus Iuris Civilis defines theft as the crime committed by someone who takes the possession of something of another, without the consent of the owner. Huguccio works on the notion of "consent" and interprets it in the light of an "urgent need of hunger."[104] In this case, it must be presumed that the owner intends to follow the obligation of the sharing of goods in case of need and does not want to be guilty of the death of the poor man. It follows that his consent must be taken as given because it is *rational* and conforms to natural law. What is *irrational* is the misrecognition of the principle according to which the earth was established in communion for all.

The right of necessity (*ius necessitatis*) does not follow the logic of the modern "right of emergency (*Notrecht*)," which Hegel understood as the right to preserve the personal living existence, even in the event of a conflict "with the rightful property of someone else."[105] The modern reasoning behind the "right of emergency" hinges on the juridical subject who, if in mortal danger, has the right to self-preservation, even if this means violating formal legal rights or the property of others. In some cases, this grammar reaches the present day. An example can be found in Article 54 of the Italian penal code: "Anyone who has been forced to commit an act due to the need to save himself or others from the real danger of serious harm to one's person, a danger not voluntarily caused by him, nor otherwise avoidable, is not punishable, provided that the fact is proportionate to the danger." It is on the basis of this article that a sentence issued on May 2, 2016, by the highest Italian Court of Appeal annulled a conviction for theft imposed on an immigrant who had stolen small quantities of food to meet the need for nourishment.[106]

This modern meaning of the *ius necessitatis* is found in Grotius, who mentions this in connection with the right to take what is necessary for one's survival.[107] There is no obligation to the poor man, but there is a benevolent exception. In medieval texts instead, *necessitatis* does not suspend existing law, because such a suspension is impossible. It is the action of the poor man in a state of necessity that gives reality and implementation to the natural law according to which things are communal (*iure naturali omnia sunt communia*). This is not a right to steal. That would still be a modern Western way of expressing the legal structure in terms of the relationship between the right of the poor man and the thing. The relationship is interpersonal and situated in a precise space-time context: The action of the poor man in a state of necessity activates the obligation of the rich man to share with the poor man. From this obligation follows the right of the poor man to take what is necessary. The whole argument focuses on duties and obligations and the restoration of a deeper level of natural law according to which *omnia sunt communia*. The rich man has duties, and his refusal to assist the hungry man must be considered murder—a crime certainly more serious than theft.[108] In the medieval conception, the just life—not life itself—is considered to be the supreme good. That is, a just life within a just order. And for this reason, the *ius necessitatis* does not only safeguard the existence of the poor man but is the call to a system of reciprocal obligations in order to restore the just order where the existing one leaves the poor man to starve. This order is to be considered, at least temporarily, unjust. If God gave life to the poor man, the rich man cannot take it away by denying him food and provisions. The *ius necessitatis* calls for a deeper legal layer to be restored.

* * *

If Luther wanted to truncate this natural law tradition—"Non est juris naturae communio rerum" (The community of goods is not in accordance with natural law)[109]—and Locke wanted to justify property as the exclusion of the common right of other men to use common land, this natural law tradition was restored and revitalized by a number of insurgents, including the Digger Winstanley in the seventeenth century and Thomas Spence in the nineteenth.[110] Now, imagine reading the texts of Locke and the Diggers synoptically. For Locke, it is right and "lawful for a man to kill a thief,"[111] whereas for Winstanley, the "power of the sword doth not only kill and rob; but by his laws, made and upheld by his power, he hedges the weak out of the earth, and either starves them or else forces them through poverty to take from others, and then hangs them for so doing. . . . This is the extremity of the curse; and yet this is the law that everyone nowadays dotes upon; when the plain truth is the law of property is the shameful nakedness of mankind."[112] In the first paragraph of the chapter "On Property" of the *Second Treatise* (1689), John Locke cites Psalm 115, verse 16: "The earth he [God] has given to mankind."[113] History would progress from this initial state to the rational state of private property through human diligence. The first line of "The True Levellers Standard Advanced" (1649) reads: "In the beginning of Time, the great Creator Reason, made the Earth to be a Common Treasury, to preserve Beasts, Birds, Fishes, and Man."[114] The human task, we read in the Diggers' text, consists of the "restoration of Israel" through "the work of making the Earth a Common Treasury."[115] The Diggers' manifesto mentions numerous passages from the Bible.[116] When John Locke, opening the *Second Treatise*, refers to biblical texts, he is implicitly opposing his arguments to those of the Diggers. On the one hand, he counterweaponized the Bible to delegitimize modern forms of common land possession and legitimize the rationality of the principle of individual private property. On the other hand, he is presenting a unilinear temporal development opposed to the temporality of the restoration claimed by the Diggers. From Locke's perspective, those who do not operate in accordance with the modern property regime are to be considered as "wild savage beasts."[117] What Locke considered as a violation of property corresponds above all to a practice of common use rights that is incompatible with the emerging legal system and the paradigm of property as "despotic dominion" over "external things of the worlds, in total exclusion of the right of any other individual in the universe."[118] In this clash of legal systems, a new form of rationality, a new experience of space, and a new concept of the world are also configured. Locke's language is symptomatic of these changes. The "wild savage beasts" correspond to the inhabitants of legal structures in which possession is in common. What must be "destroyed as a lion or a tiger" is the practice of common-use rights. This is the same colonial logic applied both within England and in the colonies. It is the war of what is defined as conforming to reason against the irrational.[119] The new legal grammar based on absolute right over external things and the exclusion of the right of others has been imposed in a long war against other forms of owning. This war has been fought through polemical and temporalized concepts that have turned anachronistic practices into something irrational, residual, savage, undisciplined, and lazy.

Locke's text does not invent anything. His texts are theoretical weapons used in the war against the commons, a war that, between the seventeenth and eighteenth centuries, evicted hundreds of thousands of commoners from forests and pastures. The polemic goal of Locke can be exemplified in a text signed by forty-five True Levellers, *A declaration from the poor oppressed people of England*: "The earth was not made purposely for you, to be Lords of it, and we to

be your Slaves, Servants, and Beggers; but it was made to be a common Livelihood to all."[120] If the practice of digging is the practice of restoring the earth as
common livelihood, Locke mobilizes theological, legal, and political arguments
in support of the long war against the commons. What emerges from this con-
frontation is not an intellectual quarrel between thinkers. I do not mean to argue
that Locke took the trouble to refute the writings of Gerrard Winstanley. What I
am arguing is that in the sixteenth and seventeenth centuries a clash took place
between alternative, competing legal systems. Locke and Winstanley expressed
that tension and took sides for different outcomes. If the Diggers refer to the
restorative temporality of common possession, which is not a past but a present
to be defended, Locke states that those common forms of ownership are survi-
vors of savages. In order to justify the right of appropriation of the land, Locke
devalues the land, transferring the valorizing potential to human activity. The
object is removed from the common natural condition through labor, which
adds something that "excludes the common right of other men."[121] Here lies the
frontal attack on the right of the commons: "If we will rightly estimate things
as they come to our use, and cast up the several expences about them, what in
them is purely owing to nature, and what to labour, we shall find, that in most of
them ninety-nine hundredths are wholly to be put on the account of labour."[122]
Human labor constitutes the title for appropriating nature that in itself, in the
Lockean view, is worth 1 percent or less.

Locke inverts terms that made sense for many hundreds of years. But it is not
Locke who makes this inversion. It operates at the basis of proprietary structures established in the early modern age. The difference between "premodern" *libertas* and modern liberty is not one of derivation but of inversion. If the
modern concept of liberty is an expansive force of the subject characterized by
a limitless appropriative tendency, *libertas* is characterized by reciprocal relations, limitations, and obligations based on relations of authority. Both must be
understood in the relationship between rights and obligations,[123] but the former
gives priority to subjective rights, the latter to obligations. Similarly, the relationship between rei-centric forms of ownership and modern forms that instead give
absoluteness to individual will should also be understood in terms of inversion.
The historical processes that led to this inversion are anything but linear.

There is a tradition that has celebrated this inversion as progress. What I want
to highlight is how the polemic nature of modern political and legal concepts
is to be read in relation to a long war between life forms and legal systems. The
long war against other ways of owning was fought both with the cannons of colonial violence organized by the state and through the canon of political thinkers

that eventually became dominant. Every concept employed by Locke and other representatives of the canon was forged in this clash and bears traces of it. It is up to a new political theory to bring this out.

* * *

Private property and absolute modern sovereignty have arisen together as two sides of the same coin. Their absoluteness refers to property "owned fully and independently by a single person"[124] and the constitutionalization of the monopoly of state power in the hands of a representative person or assembly. This process of absolutization, culminating in the French Revolution, is one of the many implications of the demarcation of the older notion of *dominium* into public power monopolized by the state and individual private property. The French Revolution and the Code Civil sanctioned this demarcation: "Property belongs to the citizen, empire to the sovereign."[125] The peak of this process can be symbolically represented by the date of August 4, 1789, with the abolition of the feudal system, which not only transformed private property into an unlimited and inalienable right but at the same time, by destroying any intermediate political authority, depoliticized the social and concentrated power in the hands of the state. This is how the Revolution shaped society.

The Code Napoléon (1804), which has served as a model for countless civil codes in many countries, not only in Europe, provides a definition of private property that has become classic: "Property is the right of enjoying and disposing of things in the most absolute manner (*La propriété est le droit de jouir et disposer des choses de la manière la plus absolue*)" (Art. 544). It was Jean-Étienne-Marie Portalis, the author of this article, who defined the right to private property by inventing a Roman origin, such as *ius utendi et abutendi* (right to use and abuse).[126] This Latin expression does not exist in Roman law. It is a modern invention that Portalis took from a work by Robert Joseph Pothier dated 1772.[127] This reinvention of Roman law allowed the projection of modern concepts onto the past, giving them an almost metahistorical character. German legal scholars worked on the definition of this concept by merging elements of the French civil code and Roman law. In the modern reading of Roman law, Georg Friedrich Puchta defined the right to property as "total power on the thing,"[128] and Ludwig Arndts defined property as "complete power over a material object."[129] Many other influential scholars could be cited. All these works refer to a modernized Roman law.

In this chapter, by referring to nonmodern practices of property within the Western and non-Western legal traditions, I wanted to show the functioning of

different legal grammars that can help us better understand alternative proprietary practices. These alternatives seem all the more necessary today as the ongoing ecological destruction becomes more severe. However, replacing a dualistic
paradigm that considers the natural world as a separate entity with a new relational, interrelational, or intrarelational paradigm is no solution, either. Adopting alternative models of interdependence and interpenetration that reject the
strict distinction between the human and the environment does not change anything in the dominant legal and economic relations that are constantly reproduced in countless everyday practices: when we sell our labor force, when we
get our salary, when we buy food or a train ticket, when we pay taxes or rent,
and even when we refuse to do so.

The process leading to ecological destruction does not lie in the dualistic
conceptions formalized in modern philosophy from Descartes to Kant or in ontological assumptions based on separation rather than relationality. The problem
has been mistakenly identified as the separation of human will and nature, as the
dualism of subject and object, the reduction of the real to calculable forces, or,
in a Heideggerian fashion, as the transformation of the forest from a sacred place
to a timber reserve. Thinking in this way means projecting a question related to
modern forms of property onto a question that spans more than two thousand
years of Western metaphysics and the history of technology. This way of thinking,
as with Heidegger, is reactionary. The question needs to be reformulated. The issue is not that humans could "turn the earth itself into a universal tool" but how
they do it, with what kinds of tools, with what kinds of social relations at work
within them.[130] The problem arises when the metabolism between humans and
nature, "common to all forms of society in which human beings live," is no longer "regulated and controlled" by communities but becomes disproportionate
because it is subjected to absolute private property and an intrinsically limitless
process of valorization. It is modern property relations that give the owner, be
it an individual or the state, the absolute right on earth.[131] As early as the 1844
Manuscripts, Marx analyzed the modern separation from nature on the basis
of the ownership and thus the possible alienation of labor power.[132] If we are
to believe that there is such a thing as a "web of life,"[133] this web is dismantled
when nature and human activity become estranged, when labor becomes wage
labor and thus estranged from the worker, i.e., someone else's property. Later,
in the first and third volumes of *Capital*, in relation to large-scale agriculture and
industry, Marx introduced the notion of the "metabolic rift (*Riß . . . des Stoff-
wechsels*)," i.e., a rupture in the material exchange between man and earth.[134]
To remedy the metabolic rift produced by modern forms of capitalist property

and production, Marx urged a "systematic restoration" of this metabolism "as a regulative law of social production."[135] It is not by conferring agency on matter that private property relations break down. Rather, it is by changing property relations that different relations with matter and humans can initiate. To paraphrase what Max Horkheimer said about fascism in 1939, it should be said today that those who do not want to talk about private property should also be silent about climate change and the environmental crisis.

In his 1844 *Manuscripts*, Marx described the suppression of private property as the basis of "truly human and social property (*wahrhaft menschliches und soziales Eigentum*),"[136] of the social man and the emancipation of human senses.[137] Social property (*soziales Eigentum*) is still a concept here. Marx used it to create a tension from which to develop critical analyses of the human relationship to the inorganic body of nature, private property, and the capitalist form of wage labor. These three concepts—nature, property, and labor—constitute a distinctive historical constellation. Their explanation requires and presupposes their connection. The practice of *propiedad social* gives substance to Marx's notion of *soziales Eigentum*. Social property is not the transfer of ownership from private hands to the state. It is the democratic control of *dominium* by users. This control transforms the structure of proprietary relations, so that ownership ceases to be absolute *dominium* over the outside world and instead becomes subject to control and limitation by a web of users. Those who work, that is, those who use their labor power and means of production, have authority over them, including what is produced, how it is produced, and under what labor relations. Similarly, a house or land abandoned by its owners is subject to democratic control for its proper use against abuse by the owners. The light of new ownership relations does not come from an imaginary future; instead, it comes from present experiments and anachronistic categories that, like *dominium utile*—a medieval concept— are capable of opening up spaces for thinking about noncapitalist ownership.

The problem today is not the excess of domination over nature and its disenchantment. The problem is, on the contrary, the deficit of dominion over the dominion relationship that governs the relationship between humans and nature. It is about reconfiguring domination in terms of conscious and democratic control over the forms of metabolism between humans and nature. Within modified social relations, quarrels and conflicts continue to take place, but they concern the qualification of what is *proper* use instead of ownership. In the case of water, but also of land and forests, the community includes the entire world. And not only the present generations but also those to come and those in the past, who have handed over to the living what they have to take care of.

The network of obligations extends spatially and temporally, to include, past, present, and future. In one of the rare foreshadowings of a "higher socioeconomic formation," Marx wrote that "the private property of single individuals in the earth will appear just as absurd as the private property of one man in other men. Even an entire society, a nation, or all simultaneously existing societies taken together, are not the owners of the earth. They are simply its possessors, its usufructuaries (*Nutznießer*), and have to bequeath it in an improved state to succeeding generations, as boni patres familias."[138] The concept of property is redefined as usufruct. Users are not owners. They take care of the land as *boni patres familias*. The notion of users goes beyond individuals, communities, and even the whole of humanity. It encompasses all of humankind, past, present, and future, and establishes bonds and obligations between generations, such as those governing the relationships of parents to children and children to parents.

If Marx prefigured other property relations by borrowing anachronistic legal categories, the notion of *dominium utile* provides a rei-centric legal structure that prioritizes relations with the thing and between users; the notion of *res nullius in bonis*, which in Roman law referred to cities or the property of God, i.e., not appropriable, can also be reanimated.[139] In this excavation it is possible to show connections between the past and the present; it is possible to extract anachronistic fragments of legal grammars for the practices of the present and for the legal construction of the future. If the parabola of possessive individualism has led to the fragmentation of the social fabric and to the use and abuse of natural resources, the solution does not lie in prioritizing community over the individual or state property over individual property. Even less can the solution to the exploitation of nature and the appropriation of the commons lie in extending the notion of legal personhood to natural entities and including them in a few articles of a constitution. A different logic is needed.

These are not ready-made solutions but rather experiments to learn from and build on with other experiments. The notion of social property, which overcomes the dichotomy between private and national property and refers instead to democratic practices, brings out the nexus between *proper use* and *democracy*. It highlights the precise point at which private property, not only in land and nature but also in the labor power of other human beings, becomes incompatible with the democracy of presence. This democracy in action, reshaping property and economic relations, exceeds the limits of democracy as contained in the representative form of the state.

3

DEMOCRACY AND THE DEMOCRATIC EXCESS

In 2009 the European Commission for Democracy Through Law (the Venice Commission) published a report on the imperative mandate. The report stated that "liberal democratic thinking established that [the] imperative mandate was incompatible with democracy" (Art. 7). The report goes on to say that the "imperative mandate is generally awkward to Western democracies" (Art. 11) and a "blatant violation of the European tradition of the free mandate of parliamentarians" (Art. 37) and concluded that the prohibition of imperative mandates "must prevail as a cornerstone of European democratic constitutionalism" (Art. 39).[1] In its most general sense, the imperative mandate is a commitment between the governors and the governed, who retain the right and authority to recall the mandataries who fail to act in accordance with the mandate given to them. It has emerged in many revolutionary events when democracy in action exceeds the limits established by "liberal democratic thinking."

In the US context, the National Conference of State Legislatures summarizes the diverging perspectives on recall in these terms: Proponents view it as a means for citizens to exercise control over elected officials, while detractors caution against its potential to foster an "excess of democracy."[2] Today, the recall process in the United States is delimited, notably precluding its use to recall members of Congress yet permitting its use against state officials in jurisdictions where it is enshrined. It was retained in the Massachusetts constitution of 1780, which stated that delegates to the US Congress would hold office for one year

and "may be recalled at any time within the year." However, this article was annulled by the adoption of the US Constitution on July 26, 1788. In US history,
Article V of the Articles of Confederation (1781) reserved power "to each State
to recall its delegates, or any of them, at any time within the year, and to send
others in their stead for the remainder of the year."[3] In 1787, when the recall
was discussed at the Constitutional Convention, Luther Martin, who was elected
to the Confederation Congress by the Maryland General Assembly, argued that
"the representatives in Congress shall be chosen annually, shall be paid by the
state, and shall be subject to recall even within the year."[4] Although considered
at the Constitutional Convention in Philadelphia, the right to recall was rejected
on the national level because recognizing the right to recall for the members of
Congress would mean recognizing that they are delegates appointed by separate,
independent sovereign states.[5]

Recently, the imperative mandate has been invoked by different political
movements. In France, not only did the right-wing Front National propose a
constitutional amendment to introduce the recall mechanism, but also the Parti
de Gauche (Left Party) mobilized to restore accountability and recall mechanisms
for elected deputies. The proposals were blocked by the majority parties as dangerous for democracy and linked with the agenda of populist movements.[6] The
issue reemerged when the Yellow Vests movement—which started in October
2018, motivated by rising fuel prices and the high cost of living—demanded the
adoption of direct democracy procedures, including the imperative mandate.
Their appeal of December 2, 2018, coincided with the establishment of local assemblies and permanently recallable representatives "with revocable imperative
mandates and with rotation of responsibilities."[7]

In Germany, the Grüne and the Pirate Party wanted to send representatives
bound by an imperative mandate to Parliament. In Spain, one of the points
in the programs of Podemos and Izquierda Unida for the June 2016 elections
concerned "the right to recall leaders who ignore electoral promises."[8] In Italy, the Five-Star Movement perceives elected representatives as spokespersons
who would lose their mandate in case of "floor crossing." Formally, the Five-Star
Movement's proposal is in contradiction to Article 67 of the Italian constitution,
which explicitly states that every representative shall carry out her/his duties
without an imperative mandate. The Five-Star Movement has instead made it
mandatary for its members of parliament to sign a contract that obliges them
to pay 250,000 Euros if they violate the Five-Star Movement's code of conduct.
Not only has it been said that this practice increases the party's control over the
elected members, but it has even been proposed to ban the Five-Star Movement
for its unconstitutional reference to the imperative mandate.[9]

The growing interest in and use of institutions such as recall should be read as a symptom of the health of current democratic institutions. In 1975, the Trilateral Commission's report "The Crisis of Democracy" warned that there was a problem of governance because of an "excess of democracy," leading to a deficit of governability.[10] The solution, according to the report's authors, was to restore a "more equitable relationship between governmental authority and popular control."[11] Today, an increasing number of states transition toward authoritarian forms without formally violating their constitutions. Parliament is being marginalized by the growing role of government, and democratic decision-making procedures are being replaced by an increasing number of executive orders. Modern constitutions are temporal devices that mark the rhythm of numerous procedures, from elections to various decision-making processes. These temporal devices are collapsing because of a growing shortage of time, which leads to a dislocation of decision-making power in the hands of the executive. It has been said that democratization and parliamentarization structurally increase the scarcity of time because they increase the number of active speakers and controversial issues to be decided.[12] A new structural dimension must be added to this one. The timeframes for the decision-making processes of the financial market are incompatibly faster than those of politics. Democratic practices are unable to catch up with them. This incompatibility between economic and constitutional time generates a sort of permanent state of temporal emergency in which decisions must be made with the speed of executive orders and not through long parliamentary discussions. If this temporal gap increases, what we will probably see in the more or less long process of implosion of the representative democratic machine is, on the one hand, a narrow government of technocrats who make decisions and, on the other, a mass of agitators and political parvenus.

Populist movements, as a symptom, can be seen both as part of the problem and as a sign of alternative ways out. In the privatization of state functions and the atomization of the social, new forms of groupings also arise. In the crisis of the democratic machine, there emerge instances, practices, and experiments with direct democracy that must be given serious consideration. Populists claim that they want to give power back to the people. From their perspective, the imperative mandate can be seen as a remedy for the lack of confidence in the representatives and the establishment. It also expresses a certain degree of dissatisfaction with the mechanisms of representative democracy and its technocrats—more broadly, as a symptom of the crisis of representative democracy. Politically, this dissatisfaction can take different forms. It can lead to authoritarian-plebiscitary democracy, bypassing these established bodies.[13] But it also can be addressed with a different kind of democratic participation articulated through intermediary bodies. These possibilities are intensified by new technologies, such as social media, which, while producing greater fragmentation, also open up new opportunities for participation and control over the production and dissemination of information and decision-making processes. However, these possibilities remain chimerical unless control is also exercised over the ownership of these technologies.

It is a question of bringing out these possibilities from the mass of morbid phenomena that characterizes the current crisis. Alternative democratic practices have emerged in countless social movements when they experience a democracy of presence. The numerous social movements that have occupied public squares, beginning with Occupy, have already presented a summary of the state of democracy. "Democracy is a joke" (Brussels), "Democracy is an illusion" (London), "Democracy has been kidnapped," said the Spanish Indignados in 2012: "We are going to save it." "Real democracy now," claimed people in different parts of the world.

Investigating democratic excess requires tracing its lineage back to the origins of the modern state, a period when its fundamental elements were still malleable. This involves reconsidering anachronistic institutions, such as the imperative mandate, in the context of the current democratic crisis. It means reviving the spirit of Machiavelli, who recognized that popular tumults are not harmful but, on the contrary, the guardian of freedom and the origin of good laws.[14]

* * *

On June 14, 1793, during the French Revolution, participants in a session of the National Convention discussed the primary assemblies' petition for the right and authority to convene spontaneously: "Art 12: Primary assemblies may be formed extraordinarily by a meeting of the majority, plus one, of their members." After a brief discussion, Robespierre stepped in to reject the article. He argued that "it would destroy all forms of government and, by excess of democracy (*par excès de démocratie*), overthrow national sovereignty."[15] Two different conceptions and practices of sovereignty confronted each other. Robespierre feared that the primary assemblies could take action against the government and, once self-convened, extend their meeting indefinitely. That was why the excess should be "tempered by laws"[16] or, in other words, caged in a constitutional shell. The way to encapsulate the excess was by suspending the constitution and killing the 1793 Declaration, arresting the *enragés*, closing their assemblies, and dissolving the Société des républicaines révolutionnaires (Society of Revolutionary Republican Women). In other words, *Terror*. Terror is not an expression of the excess but, on the contrary, of the war against it. *Enragés* and women were accused of counterrevolutionary activities, with the aggravating circumstance, for women, of violating their naturally ordained civic duty, that is, taking care of the home and family.[17] Often liberals, but not only, think that the excess is manifested in the abuses of the state and the police. They think that the excess is a kind of violence that can only generate more violence. Others think that it is a violence necessary to preserve the results of the revolution. These positions are symmetrical and often overlap and coincide in the minds of those who represent them. They all assume the point of view of the state whose power is to be contained or intensified and directed according to supposedly better ends.

James Madison feared and wanted to marginalize "unpropertied masses."[18] He was also averse to a plurality of powers and the recall of members of Congress by individual states. He saw that such a plurality was incompatible with the constitutional logic of the modern state, stating, "Two Sovereignties can not co-exist within the same limits."[19] Consistent with this assumption, Madison affirmed that "the general power whatever be its form if it preserves itself, must swallow up the State powers. Otherwise, it will be swallowed up by them."[20] These assumptions express nothing other than the constitutional grammar of the modern representative state: Since the people cannot act collectively, representation is made necessary, and what has to be represented are not conflicting local interests but "the whole over its parts."[21] If the sovereign is such, he has no powers above himself. And if the sovereign represents the whole people, there are not even local powers capable of containing that power. Having eliminated the counterpowers capable of balancing the representative power of the whole, the only way forward is the containment of this new absolute power within the mechanisms of checks and balances. Both Alexander Hamilton in the American Revolution and Robespierre in the French Revolution defined the "dispersion" of sovereignty in terms of an excess of democracy.[22]

Democracy, Rancière observed, is a transgression of limits, a disproportion that provokes fear and even hatred.[23] Democracy changes the rules for ordering the existing order. Hence the rarity of politics.[24] But it is not only a disruptive event that challenges the existing order without being an order itself. The latter, when it challenges the state order, is not created out of nothing but is the result of the reconfiguration of social institutions and past legal traditions. Democratic excess does not bring disorder but instead a different order, which may be incompatible with the dominant one. What really disturbs those who oppose excess is found in the etymology of the word. The Latin *excessus*, from *ex*, "out," and *cedere*, "to go, yield," denotes a departure, a way out, a going beyond certain established boundaries. In the cases considered, this is a departure from the grammar of the state. For this reason, Robespierre's concern was also shared by the Girondins, according to whom the unity and indivisibility of national sovereignty had to be safeguarded since it belonged to the whole people and not to primary assemblies.[25] Condorcet had devised a number of constitutional mechanisms to ensure that the active portion of citizens would cease "to appear as the whole people."[26]

The democratic excess worried not only Robespierre and Condorcet at the moment of France's revolution. Both liberals and conservatives are intimidated by it. When Hannah Arendt discusses civil disobedience, she is careful to find a "constitutional niche" that can contain it.[27] Carl Schmitt was no less fearful of the democratic excess; he sought to overturn it into the "undemocratic element" that operates in the heart of modern democratic states.[28] Since its origins, modern political theory has been configured as a war against excess. Excess has been pushed into the state of nature and counterposed to the civil state; it has been equated with chaos and counterposed to order, assimilated to a condition dominated by the fear of violent death and counterposed to the fear of power and the state monopoly to kill, and associated with instability and counterposed to the stability of the law. These and other binary oppositions provide the foundation for the fundamental concepts of the modern state.

The excess, when it surfaces, or when it breaks the shell in which liberals and conservatives would like to encapsulate it, dis-orders the existing order and challenges the structure that constitutes its scaffold. This clash gives rise not only to a more or less violent police and military reaction but also to a reaction in the field of theory. The many insurgencies that took place in France between 1831 and 1834 saw the red flag emerge on the barricades of Lyon alongside the French flag. The insurgency shattered the dream of national unity and homogeneity and the idea of a *peuple* celebrated by Jules Michelet. These events provoked a violent military and theoretical reaction. Tocqueville referred to the revolution of 1848 as a shock that "had reduced society itself to dust."[29] Cohesion and national unity were shattered: "One aimed at destroying inequality of fortune, another inequality of education, a third undertook to do away with the oldest of all inequalities, that between man and woman."[30] Inequalities imply binaries to be preserved: those between wealth and poverty, between civilized and barbarian, and that between the sexes. To stabilize women's necessary dependence on men, Jules Michelet moved toward the naturalization of the separation between reproductive function and rational management of the state, concluding: "Man is the brain, woman the uterus."[31] In 1792, when the women of the French Revolution claimed a revolutionary citizenship based on their social and political participation, the deputy of the Legislative Assembly replied that if these claims were honored, "the order of nature would be inverted."[32] The history of the naturalization of fundamental concepts of the modern social order is a reaction to the many insurgencies that have challenged the social and political order built on the binaries of public/private, communal property/private property, individual/state, alien/citizen, male/female. Modern thinkers usually picture women "as an excess to be contained, in the interests of political and moral life, primarily through the restriction of the woman to the private realm of the household under the dominion of her father and/or husband. To be a woman was by definition to be excluded from participation in the political domain."[33]

The insurgents, that is, the theorists of an alternative canon, have paid a high price for their theory in action. For challenging the existing proprietary order, the separation of public and private (including gender), and the nation-state, the Communards, after being slaughtered, were downgraded to inferior, pathologically criminal human beings; the insurgent women were defined as *pétroleuses*, incendiaries, "drunken Bacchants, hysterical Messalinas dancing around a Spahi, 'the black devil'—a round of infernal witches."[34] The reports of the trials of the Communards "stressed the physical anomalies or deformities of the women,"[35] and Cesare Lombroso, by looking at fifty photographs of Communards, found that eleven showed some anomalies and 47 percent in general were composed of criminal and inferior types.[36] During the trials of the Communards, Captain Jouenne defined the Commune as a "horrible campaign against civilization."[37] All these forms of pathologization should be read as a reaction against insurgent practices that challenged the existing order. The definition of some subjects as pathological is not the consequence of a new episteme that divides the normal from the pathological, for this division is the continuation in the theory of police reaction to insurgent practices that dis-order the dominant order. In the nineteenth century, when the existing order was shaken to its foundations by new social rebellions, the reaction was the preservation of the order through its naturalization and the pathologization of the insurgents as opponents of the natural order.

My aim is not to investigate the war against democratic excess from the perspective of the state and the dominant canon. Instead, I am interested in exploring the theory and practice of an alternative canon rooted in historical examples and institutions capable of articulating democratic excess. The imperative mandate, grounded in a plurality of powers, the dispersion of sovereignty, and the control of rulers, serves as a privileged lens through which to examine democracy when it surpasses the established legal framework of the modern state.

* * *

The *mandatum imperativum* is an institution of medieval origin in which representative deputies, or mandataries, have a bond of mandate; that is, they receive instructions and can be recalled by their electors for failing to follow these instructions. These deputies are not considered to be individuals with the right to vote but rather as members of assemblies of estates and local communities. Traces of this institution can be found in many political arrangements.[38] The tradition of the imperative mandate runs parallel to the constitutional history of modern states, not only in Europe. Progressively banned by numerous modern constitutions, especially after the French Revolution's affirmation of the modern principle of the unity of national sovereignty, the imperative mandate has often been stigmatized as an anachronism to be dismissed, a font of confusion, a temporal obstacle in the decision-making process, incompatible with the idea of national representation, which is the basis of the modern state.

The imperative mandate functions as a prism capable of showing a political and legal structure to be made up of a plurality of authorities. These authorities, in the Middle Ages, did not derive from the public power of the crown but were founded on anterior rights of local communities. Not even the *regnum* can be conceived as an expression of the unitary power of the crown; instead, it is a composite body of associations, privileged bodies, and customary practices. In this regard, the Middle Ages offers not a model but an example that shows another way of practicing politics, law, and possession.[39] The imperative mandate must be understood in the pluralist context, in which authority is not concentrated in the hands of the state but dispersed in a multiplicity of local communities. Authority and rights are not the emanation of a central power but have an autonomous origin and reside within corporate groups. Categories such as public law and private law, but also international law and criminal law, are not only inappropriate for understanding this pluralist context; what is more, if such categories are used, they alter the pluralist context, turning it into a kind of immature and confused image of Western political and legal modernity.[40]

In the medieval practice of imperative mandate, each procurator represented only the municipality that granted him his mandate. *Mandatum imperativum* was binding on the deputy, and the elected deputies consulted with their fellow nobles to be well informed and receive instructions.[41] In the case of medieval

Spain, the system was based on the authority of municipalities and *concejos*, councils, which controlled the representative's power of decision so that, when "the procurator spoke, it was the voice of Zamora or Seville, Salamanca or Cordova."[42] The procurator, following instructions, acted as a local agent and not as a representative of the nation as a whole.[43] And the procurator assumed the entire risk of being spokesman (*porte-paroles*), as happened to "Roderigo de Tordesillas, procurator of Segovia, who was arraigned by his community because he voted without power or authority for a subsidy asked by the Crown in the Cortes of Coruña in 1520. Adjudged guilty, he was dragged ignominiously through the streets by a rope around his neck, and later was hanged by the feet."[44] It is best not to be upset by the violence and instead follow the legal and political grammar that underlies the imperative mandate.

The mandatary answers to the authority of a local assembly whose power is independent from the power of the crown. To avoid easy analogies with the modern model of the federal state, it is necessary to emphasize some substantial differences. The sovereignty involved in the practice of the imperative mandate is dispersed and not represented in the unity of a president or assembly; the social is politically articulated in a plurality of authorities and communities, not atomized individuals. If the mandataries could be punished, it is because they had obligations and duties. In the medieval context, the term right, *ius*, was semantically connected to justice and the use of force to preserve or restore it—which is what happens in the case of the punishment of a mandatary. In Althusius, who was one of the last champions of the monarchomachist tradition in early modernity, the imperative mandate and the right of resistance were parts of the same legal framework and designed in relation to associations and orders. This context was characterized by an interplay of powers: people, the supreme magistrate, and the *ephors*, who acted as an intermediate political power and could exercise the *jus gladii*, the "right of the sword" against tyrannical abuse of the supreme magistrate.[45] If modern legal categories were to be used, all this would appear chaotic, like the collapse of the rule of law and of every system of checks and balances.

Edmund Burke's affirmation in his *Speech to the Electors of Bristol* of November 1774 is explicitly mentioned in the European "Report on the Imperative Mandate" and often taken as an example of the incompatibility between the modern state and the imperative mandate: "Parliament is a deliberative assembly of *one* nation, with *one* interest, that of the *whole*; where, not local purposes, not local prejudices ought to guide, but the general good, resulting from the general reason of the whole. You choose a Member, indeed; but when you have chosen him, he is not Member of Bristol, but he is a Member of Parliament."[46] These statements show the transition from a way of understanding representatives as defenders of the interests of individual communities and localities to a way of understanding representation of the whole. If, in the medieval legal tradition, commons considered their representatives as inherently obliged to increase their liberties,[47] then in the process of consolidation of the modern state and its *plena potestas*, the representatives assumed the new function of representatives of "*one* nation, with *one* interest, that of the *whole*." In this new framework, there is no place for instructions or mandates.

If the parliament is the deliberative assembly of one, whole nation, the representation of the unity of the nation is not compatible with the imperative mandate, which is instead the expression of local sovereign assemblies and districts. Indeed, in almost all European constitutions the imperative mandate is explicitly forbidden, for the deputies do not represent their party or particular interests but the nation as a whole, which is "superior of and different from local constituencies."[48] If each representative represents the whole nation, it is evident that, strictly speaking, she/he cannot be revoked by a part of it.

Emile Durkheim once explained that if, on the one hand, the imperative mandate expresses the widespread feelings of the collective, then on the other, "nothing can be more contrary, in some respects, to the very notion of democracy."[49] He should have added "representative." The discourse is about representative democracy within the framework of the modern state, not democracy per se. Schmitt would have agreed that the imperative mandate "contradicts the idea of political unity as well as the fundamental presupposition of democracy."[50] It is a process that has characterized the vicissitudes, albeit at different times, of many European states. If we take the point of view of the state and express ourselves through the grammar of the modern representative state that arose in Europe, all the objections to the imperative mandate are correct. Indeed, the explicit prohibition of the imperative mandate is a consequence of the constitutional structure of the Western modern nation-state. The imperative mandate is forbidden because it is logically incompatible with the representation of the nation that, in its totality, is the real bearer of sovereignty. Indeed, in the case of the imperative mandate, the mandatary depends on instructions and directions from the voters, from individual electoral districts, and not "the people as unity."[51]

It is not a question of understanding the imperative mandate as a democratic corrective for the lack of trust in the establishment. Instead, it is a question of marking the difference and incompatibility between the modern representative system and the constitutional implications of the imperative mandate.

What Schmitt understands is that democratic excess cannot be imprisoned in a system of checks and balances. If the excess has a centrifugal tendency toward the dispersion and pluralization of power, the representative mechanism has an opposite centripetal function toward unity. However, the excess cannot really be bottled up. But it can be channeled into the "undemocratic element" encapsulated in the heart of the modern state: "For the representative quality contains the undemocratic element (*das Nichtdemokratische*) in this democracy."[52] This undemocratic element contained in the representative democracy is the *unity* of the nation-state understood as a *whole* people. As Hobbes had already pointed out, unity exists only as represented: A "multitude of men, are made One Person, when they are by one Person, represented. . . . For it is the unity of the representor, not the unity of the represented, that maketh the person one."[53] In more democratically inclined thinkers, such as Locke, the representative mechanism can be mediated by the idea of trust and the regular periodicity of elections; however, both Locke and Hobbes cannot disregard the centrality of representation, and both share the same emphasis on unity: Men "enter into society to make *one* people *one* body politic under *one* supreme government."[54] This is the core of modern political theology investigated by Carl Schmitt. The centrifugal force of the pluralism of the democratic excess is restrained by the centripetal force of the unity of the "undemocratic element," which, according to Schmitt, has to channel the possible dispersion of sovereignty toward the unity embodied by a monarch, president, or Führer. Today, an increasing number of so-called liberal democracies, whether or not they enact substantial constitutional reforms, are placing more and more powers in the hands of a president directly elected by the people.

Liberal-democrat theorists who oppose the democratic excess and the imperative mandate are actually on the same side as the legal scholar Carl Schmitt and his political theology. It is this proximity that irritates and makes liberal thinkers uncomfortable when confronted with Schmitt. His political theology was only prima facie the transfer of religious concepts into the political concepts of the modern theory of the state, so that "the omnipotent God became the omnipotent lawgiver."[55] From this superficial perspective, the analogy concerns the absoluteness of power, which goes from being an attribute of God to becoming an attribute of the sovereign that was previously limited by a concrete *ordo* of *auctoritates*, customs and divine law. But there is a second, deeper layer of this political theology. The idea of popular sovereignty, which is specifically related to the conception of the democratic state, points to an element of transcendence that Schmitt, following Hobbes, shows to be at the heart of the modern conception of the state. Indeed, the people, as a sovereign subject, must be put into form; their unity and totality must be created by the unity of the representative. In other words, Schmitt observes, the people as unity does not exist until it is made visible by representation: "To represent means to make an invisible being visible (*sichtbar machen*) and present through a publicly present one."[56] The people, as a singular political subject, is the absent that becomes present and visible through the representative who acts in the name of the people and transforms the multitude into a unity. The president is not a tinsel of the state but one who, in the singularity of his person, makes visible the unity of the people in the name of which he speaks and acts. It is in the logic of representation, of making visible what is invisible, that the true nature of political theology nestles. The imperative mandate is incompatible with this political logic. It occurred in historical and political contexts in which the sovereign power was limited by plural authorities, and it has reappeared every time the unity and the monopoly of power by the state has been broken and limited by a pluralism of powers, assemblies, districts, councils, and soviets, whose power is distributed both horizontally and vertically. They control and can revoke their mandataries, which control and limit the government through the horizontal powers of assemblies. It is the power of many units against unity.

* * *

There is a link "between the abolition of privately owned public power and the creation of undivided national sovereignty."[57] With the 1789 decree on the abolition of the feudal order, property became an absolute and individual title, putting an end to the splitting of property rights over a given piece of real estate, on the one hand, and destroying the multiple strata of lords who exercised local police powers, on the other. These processes are not unilinear but characterized by the intertwining of at least three different temporalities. Looking at the revolutionary process from its outcomes, what I call reverse teleology, the feudal order, founded on dependence and hierarchy, is destroyed because it is incompatible with the modern principles of freedom and equality. Looking at a more extended temporality, the destruction of the feudal order can be considered part of the consolidation of an absolute and undivided national sovereignty.[58] The revolution accelerates and completes the work begun by the absolute monarchy in the Ancien Régime. This process is accomplished by depoliticizing the social. However, if the demarcation process is observed from the point of view of the democratic excess of unsynchronized historical agents, not only does a different story emerge but also a different vision of history. Anachronisms emerge that interrupt and reconfigure the present. And the *reactive* nature of modern political and juridical concepts emerges as well.

During the French Revolution, the peasants of the provinces took part in the revolution by attacking nobles and "castles, burning property records, taking redistributive measures."[59] Here is the other insurgent temporality. On the night of August 4, 1789, the decree was discussed under the urgency of a report on the disorder on the provinces and countryside. The report stated that "letters from all the provinces indicate that property of all kinds is a prey to the most criminal violence; on all sides chateaux are being burned, convents destroyed, and farms abandoned to pillage. The taxes, the feudal dues, all are extinct; the laws are without force, and the magistrates without authority."[60] While the mobilization of rural communities pushed the Constituent Assembly to make "antifeudal" decisions, because antifeudalism was already in place in the practice of the peasants, the rural insurgency was "fundamentally anti-capitalistic in scope and aimed at protecting existing communitarian structures."[61] It follows that the revolution was open to different outcomes and not necessarily aimed at the privatization of land ownership. The so-called bourgeois outcome did not incorporate peasant aspirations but was rather a reaction against them in order to neutralize them. The attack on the political property of the church and other bodies, its transfer into private individual property, was one of the tools used to neutralize the local authority not only of *seigneuries* but of corporations, communities, and parishes. It was part of the long war to impose a new social and legal order aimed at breaking the peasants' alternative legal practices. It is significant that the peasants "felt their liberty increasingly restricted—more so . . . in 1848, than before 1789."[62]

Before being explicitly forbidden in the postrevolutionary 1791 French constitution,[63] the monarch had already opposed the practice of the imperative mandate. In June 1789, Louis XVI opposed the mandates of the representatives of the three orders gathered in the National Assembly: "His Majesty declares that in subsequent meetings of the États généraux he will not suffer *cahiers* or *mandats* to ever be regarded as imperative: they must be considered as mere instructions entrusted to the conscience and free opinion of the deputies who will make their decision."[64] The *cahiers de doléances* were indeed instructions through which the États, thanks to their authority, bound their representatives. The king, freeing the members of the National Assembly from mandates, made them "free" from instructions, binding, and all authority that was not that of the monarch himself.

The abolition of the imperative mandate is a consequence of the neutralization of the authority of intermediary bodies and the process of concentration of power started by the absolute monarchies and constitutionally perfected by the French Revolution. As Tocqueville observed, the concentration of power in the hands of the National Assembly had given birth to a power that was "more extensive, more minute, and more absolute" than the power that previous kings had ever exercised.[65] To reach this "more absolute" power it was necessary to take a further "democratic" step: voting by head count, through which the intermediate bodies were broken down into a multiplicity of individual atoms. Sièyes was the spokesman for this motion: "For the deputy there is, and can be, no binding mandate, indeed no positive expression of will, but the national will."[66] Similarly, the Girondin Jacques Thouret affirmed that the triumph of the imperative mandate would mean the triumph of local interests and, hence, the collapse of the entire representative system. The Girondin emphasis on the indivisibility of sovereignty, which would lie not in some "partial union of citizens" but in the "whole nation,"[67] was no less than that of the Jacobins. Robespierre agreed with affirming the incompatibility between the imperative mandate and national representation.

This new trajectory was set in motion by many government interventions. One of the most important was proposed by Le Chapelier and passed by the National Assembly vote on June 14, 1791. The first article declared the "abolition of any kind of citizen's guild in the same trade or of the same profession. . . . It is forbidden to reestablish them under any pretext or in any form whatsoever."[68] And Article 4 declared that "if citizens belonging to the same professions, craft, or trade have joint discussion and make joint decisions . . . then the said deliberations and agreements . . . shall be declared unconstitutional, derogatory to liberty and the declaration of the rights of man."[69] These rights of man appropriated by the state were used against the insurgent rights of man of the assemblies. The Le Chapelier law was a declaration of war against guilds and corporations: On one side were local authorities, municipal liberties, and the rights of groups; on the other was the constitution of the modern state and its monopoly of power, individual freedom, and the right of the atomistic "man." The battle that Le Chapelier waged against corporate structures as forms of economic and political association of workers was both legal and temporal. "There are no longer corporations in the state, there is *no longer* anything but the particular interest of each individual, and the general interest. It is permitted to no one to inspire an intermediary interest in citizens, to separate them from the public interest by a spirit of corporation."[70] Power cannot be dispersed at the level of social bodies, which, as Le Chapelier reiterated, belonged to the archaic Ancien Régime. The march of progress is marked by the state, and the revolution obtains its legitimacy through the authority of progress, in whose name the state shapes society. What is opposed to it is an anachronism without authority.

An alternative emerged in the practice of assemblies. In 1792, the *enragé* Jean-François Varlet presented to the Convention nationale a pamphlet on the imperative mandate, in which he advocated sovereignty to the primary assemblies and sections, in which the people actually assembled and discussed, controlled, and tabulated orders to the mandataries. He challenged the grammar of representation: "Deputies, you will no longer be our representatives, you will be our mandataries, our organ."[71] He continued by saying, "In drafting our mandate, we did not worry about whether this procedure was followed by all the sections of free France. It was enough for us to know that we had the right to do it."[72] The assemblies were acting as sovereign assemblies, and, by doing so, they were practicing a different conception of sovereignty, which split unity into a plurality of powers. It is this plurality of powers that worries liberal thinkers because, instead of neutralizing conflict, it accepts conflict as an intrinsic dimension of politics. The main trajectory of the French Revolution culminated in the Terror, which was the state's attempt to synchronize the country, to crush the old regime's plurality of intermediary bodies and assemblies in the name of unity, to dismantle the medieval imperative mandate in the name of the modern principle of the free mandate of parliamentarians, to demolish backward institutions of the Ancien Régime in the name of progress, to impose new property relations. In other words, it was a gigantic attempt to synchronize many temporalities within the revolution and the country. If, as already noted, the process of demarcation produced the separation between the monopoly of public power and individual private property, between state and society, the legal monism of the state and its monopoly of state power can only be challenged by simultaneously challenging modern private property relations. In other words, real legal pluralism can only flourish beyond the modern concept of private property and its absoluteness enshrined in *ius utendi et abutendi*. This is a step that conservatives and liberals dare not take.

* * *

The imperative mandate emerged countless times in the revolutionary processes of modernity. The imperative mandate was restored in the French Revolution when, on November 18, 1789, the district of Prémontrés declared that "the imperative mandate is . . . a principle of natural law (*mandat impératif est . . . un principe de droit naturel*)."[73] It was restored in the *enragés*' appeal for the imperative mandate and primary assemblies as the source of popular sovereignty.[74] It was restored again when the Communards of 1871 referred to the "communal idea of the twelfth Century" to reactivate the imperative mandate, the "legacy of the ancient communes and the French Revolution."[75] Its tradition emerged again in the practice of the assemblies and the councils' republic in the German revolution and in the Zapatistas' practice of *mandar obedeciendo*.

These examples show the presence of a legacy that emerges not only when discontent and distrust of the establishment increases but when the democratic excess interrupts the dominant temporality of the nation-state and makes seemingly anachronistic institutions emerge. In light of these traditions, the imperative mandate is an archaic residue, but seen otherwise, it expresses a new possible configuration of our political institutions. Indeed, what is obsolete today is the representative state democracy. There are anachronistic institutions that contain possible futures, which are still encapsulated in what-has-been.[76] Several times, the medieval institution of the imperative mandate has been reactivated in new forms. It always showed us other possible trajectories of modernity. Indeed, Western political modernity was not the necessary outcome of the dissolution of the Middle Ages. There were other ways offered to configure the enormous corpus of the Middle Ages' legal, political, and economic material. The imperative mandate shows possible trajectories, ones not based on the representation of the nation as a unified political entity. First, it establishes a tension with the dominant temporality of the nation-state, and in the tension produced, it unfolds a new field of possibilities for the present. Second, by interrupting the dominant temporality, it also gives rise to a different temporalization of the historical elements, so that the Middle Ages not only ceases to be a *middle* age but also ceases to be relegated to the past, which allows us to look at it in a new way—neither with reactionary nostalgia nor with the pride of the guardians of civilization. Its otherness transforms it into a rich arsenal of legal forms and political and economic institutions alternative to the dominant ones. Far from being a dark age, it becomes a source of light capable of illuminating alternatives to the dominant Western modernity. From this perspective, the "Middle Ages" becomes the name for a legal and social order incompatible with modern Western legal and political categories.

The legacy of the imperative mandate escapes the modern political dualism based on the opposition of represented-representative and reactivates, at the least, a tripartite political structure in which the governed check their representatives, who are not the holders of sovereignty but who act according to mandates and exercise a power that is limited by the power of the governed. This is not a constitutional division of power, which in the context of modern constitutionalism remains "one power": the power of the sovereign people gathered in the nation. Instead, it is a *pluralism of powers* that questions the monopoly of power of the state. This is the real political challenge of democracy, which emerges only if we do not identify the demos with the nation, as populist movements tend to do by building a series of binary oppositions between a "we" and a "they," which essentially reflects the friend-enemy logic and runs within the framework of the modern nation-state.[77] In the trajectory of council democracy and the imperative mandate, instead of concentrating power in the hands of the state, power is dispersed into a plurality of powers. In this plurality the democratic excess, which modern constitutionalism seeks to tame, can express itself. That excess holds open the political form and does not neutralize conflict. Democracy does not have to do with a constitutional form and procedures but with that excess, with the possibility of dis-ordering the existing order and reinventing new institutional frameworks. Even if this may generate instability. This is the virtuous instability that derives from politics and, therefore, from the possibility of conflict, or, as Machiavelli would have put it, the tumults that characterize freedom and disputes over justice.

* * *

The political modernity of the state can be defined as a gigantic reaction against the manifestations of the democratic excess. It is the enormous attempt to neutralize conflicts, to create order and unity through exclusions, separations, oppositions, and binaries. In its obsession with unity, modern democracy survives by virtue of the "undemocratic element" contained in the heart of the state. Today it is clear that the price to pay for stability, security, and unity is too high. An authoritarian turn that involves an increasing number of states is visible to everyone. Constitutional mechanisms and the rule of law can be systematically suspended in the name of national emergencies and public safety. However, the *demos* keeps finding new ways to make its voice heard and express its dissatisfaction with decision-making mechanisms that appear increasingly distant and impersonal. The representative machine of the modern state operates under the assumption that the sovereign people can be put to sleep while the representatives act on their behalf and in their interests. The sovereign people are awakened once every two or more years and called upon, not as a collective but as a collection of serial individuals, to express their opinion on who will represent them during their next years of sleep. Yet the *demos* always finds ways to intervene and take the political stage. It is akin to the republican festival that Rousseau also discussed in his *Letter to d'Alembert on the Theatre*. Spectators, wrote Rousseau, "become an entertainment to themselves"; they become "actors themselves."[78] The theater is not empty like Hobbes's. It is filled. But the audience is not the educated audience sitting in the auditorium judging an actor's actions. The audience takes the stage.

People want to be actors and authors. Their taking of the floor, through new media and other information channels, is indicative of a possible new democratic practice that goes beyond the form of representative democracy. Fearful of unleashing the excess, the guardians of representative democracy are distrusting of citizens taking an active role in the legislative process: Citizens may not be sufficiently informed, or they are often guided by biased interests. It's a long story. At the beginning of the twentieth century, when progressive forces in the United States pushed for the introduction of forms of direct democracy such as recall and initiative, the *Los Angeles Times* expressed its disapproval by talking about "ignorance and caprice and irresponsibility of the multitudes."[79] This distrust and fear of the masses is hard to quell.[80]

If the dominant canon of political theory seeks to encapsulate the democratic excess, an alternative canon should be liberated from the obsession with unity and create space for the excess. This means that we must learn to live with some degree of instability. Or, in other words, we must learn to be truly democratic.[81] It means thinking and practicing politics in terms of pluralism. It is about restoring the political fabric of the social, that is, its multiplicity of institutions and local authorities capable of exercising real democratic control over both representative bodies and what is used in common.

* * *

In the United States, although the term "imperative mandate" was rarely used at the end of the nineteenth century,[82] nineteen US states currently have provisions for the recall of elected officials. The imperative mandate does not coincide with the right of recall, which is the "device that allows voters to discharge and replace a public official."[83] Among the numerous objections directed against the recall—often converging with a generic distrust of the competence of the population—the main opposition concerned its incompatibility with the principles of the modern representative state, especially if the recall was extended to a member of the Senate or the House of Representatives. An opponent of the referendum and recall wrote that a municipality and town charters cannot make themselves "an *imperium in imperio*, acting over the head of the regularly established State government."[84] This statement suggests two things: The first concerns the incompatibility between the sovereign state and the plurality of powers at the base of the recall; the second concerns a change of scale. Individual states would no longer recall representatives, but rather municipalities would claim this right. Indeed, Populists and the Socialist Labor Party in the 1880s tried to introduce radical tools of direct democracy.[85] Among its political demands, the Socialist Labor Party's platform (1896) contained some elements that referred to the more radical tradition of the imperative mandate. Along with the people's right "to propose laws and to vote upon all measures of importance, according to the referendum principle," the socialist platform also claimed the principle of "municipal self-government."[86] This was Oberholtzer's polemical goal when he wrote that a municipality cannot make itself an *imperium in imperio*. This is where recall can become what Oberholtzer feared, i.e., a tool "to attack the representative system through the machinery of direct government."[87]

Oberholtzer was right. The logic of the imperative mandate undermines the principle of indivisible sovereignty. The imperative mandate is not a referendum. The difference should be clear. Both on the right and on the left. When Antonio Gramsci referred to a system of workshop delegates as an assembly in which "the delegate is elected by a work squad, imperatively mandated, and instantly recallable,"[88] he distanced himself from the referendum. The referendum neutralizes the political articulation of collectivities structured in councils and assemblies and replaces it with the image of the people made up of atomized individuals. In a referendum, the majority of citizens respond individually and with secret suffrage to a question already posed. This means that the mass of citizens continues to act as a depoliticized mass to make the smallest possible decision—a yes or a no—on a decision already made.[89]

On the opposing front, Carl Schmitt argued that a referendum does not express any form of direct democracy because it is always a "people" of isolated individuals acting through an electoral procedure predefined by the constitution, who answer a question formulated not by the "people" but by an organized minority. If you are looking for the direct presence of the "people," Schmitt went on, it can be found in the "acclamation" of the political leader and in the "political awareness of identification and unity" with him.[90] The acclamation of and identification with a leader is the right-wing response to the crisis of the state, to the depoliticization and atomization of the social. For the rest, the "directness of democracy cannot be organized without ceasing to be direct."[91] This means that the institutions of so-called direct democracy, such as referendums and initiatives, are procedures already mediated and guaranteed by the constitution. The people do not act as a constituent power but are dispersed in a mass of voters subordinated to the constitutional rules, which remain the only true objectified expression of the constituent power of the people as unity.

The imperative mandate, instead, recalls another way of practicing politics, one based neither on atomized individuals nor on the unitary concept of people as a nation but on a plurality of groups, associations, and assemblies. For this reason, it differs from the referendum, and for the same reason, if taken seriously, it constitutes a step toward the undoing of the modern principle of national sovereignty. Politics based on groups, associations, and assemblies, such as that experienced in numerous events that have characterized the legacy of insurgent universality—from the assemblies of the sans-culottes to the councils of the twentieth century—should also make it possible to overcome the dualism between constituent power and constituted power. Indeed, if, as in the historical cases mentioned in this chapter, the democratic excess is distributed into already existing institutions and assemblies, the constituent power ceases to be a mythical dimension of the power of the people and manifests itself, instead, in already constituted alternative forms to state power. Constituent power exists only as it is already represented by those who act in its name and write the constitution. In other words, it exists as a founding myth. Its temporality is the future perfect tense. The temporality of the democratic excess is instead the present continuous. It exists as it is visible in what assemblies and associations are doing in the everyday temporality of political life.

It is a question of changing direction and following the theoretical anticipations contained in the practice of the insurgents when they open futures stuck in the past, when they reactivate the imperative mandate, when they explicitly refer to the past to configure new democratic institutions and practices. At this point it is necessary to be clear about the implications of the imperative mandate. It can be tamed in a confederation as the right of individual states to remove their representatives from a national assembly; it can be anesthetized and controlled by establishing percentages and thresholds of voters in a referendum. But if it is true that the "recall is in many respects the most controversial of direct democracy practices,"[92] we can go further, to the point of emphasizing its incompatibility with the system of the representative state.[93] Landauer provides the right starting point. The reactivation of the imperative mandate takes place in a revolutionary trajectory that returns "to the true democracy we can

find in the medieval constitutions of municipalities and provinces."[94] The reference here to the medieval institution of the imperative mandate constitutes the
springboard for jumping into a future that is not teleologically preordered by
historical stages to be passed through. If the Social Democrats saw the Bavarian
and Berlin insurgencies as a storm doomed to failure because the time was not
yet ripe for socialism, the insurgents saw in their own practices real anticipations
of different forms of political, social, and economic life. But Landauer, differentiating between a politics of "atomized voters abdicating their power," on the
one hand, and "municipalities, cooperatives, and associations determining their
own destiny in big assemblies,"[95] on the other, had indicated a further step. That
differentiation undermined the modern demarcation according to which there
would be the political state, on the one hand, and a mass of private individuals,
on the other.

In the case of the imperative mandate, Schmitt writes, "the deputy's dependence on the instructions and directions of the voters, would, indeed, eliminate
the representative character of the popular assembly, and yet it would not be an
appropriate means for the execution of the democratic principle. For it would
also contradict the political idea of democracy itself."[96] Which concept of democracy? The contradiction that Schmitt identifies between democracy and the
imperative mandate is illuminating: He overlaps the concept of representative
democracy with that of the unity of the people. The imperative mandate breaks
the circularity of the modern democratic state; thus what is being represented
is the "political unity as a whole," which exists not as something present but
only as re-presented.[97] This is precisely what occurred in the practice of the
Cochabamba insurgents, when they drew a distinction between the "simulation
of democracy" and the "democracy of presence."[98] In the representative democracy, if it is the unity of the whole that must be represented, the "tendency of
the parts to encroach on the authority of the whole"[99] must be marginalized. If
the individual representatives are responsible to the whole, then free mandate
and unaccountability must prevail. At the basis of the imperative mandate there
would instead be the real presence of a plurality of groups, parts, and councils.
Schmitt's conclusion on the imperative mandate is that it "contradicts the idea
of political unity as well as the fundamental presupposition of democracy."[100]
But if the plurality of local groups, forms of self-government, and authority presents itself as a configuration incompatible with the principles of the modern
representative state, it is precisely this incompatibility that opens theoretical
and practical space for other political and institutional trajectories. It is these
trajectories that have emerged in countless political events, past and present,

and that have made these current reflections possible. From the point of view of the modern concept of the state, the imperative mandate is an anachronism that contradicts its foundations; that is, it contradicts the notion of people as unity and totality, on which the last and most exclusive status privilege, that of citizenship, takes shape.

4

CITIZENSHIP AND SANCTUARY

In 2008, a text entitled *The Role of Sanctuary in an Insurgency* was published by the US School of Advanced Military Studies.[1] It covers the history of the relationship between insurgency and sanctuary from the Napoleonic wars in Spain, to the anticolonial struggles, up to "Zapatista's social, virtual, and legal sanctuaries."[2] The text investigates cases of "insurgent sanctuaries" in order to defeat, mitigate, and contain them.[3] Its aim is to outline strategies against "terrorist organizations," which constitute "a threat to international peace and prosperity," and in this perspective the sanctuaries are examined as places of refuge for the ideologies and resources of the insurgents. The overall meaning of the text, written and to be read in the light of the US Patriot Act, is an attack on every "refuge" intended as a real or virtual place removed from state control, from the medieval *fuero* used in the Spanish guerrilla warfare against Napoleonic troops, to the Chiapas of the Zapatistas, to any legal autonomy from state power. Although the text is crude, it well expresses the point of view of the state as provided by the Patriot Act, which "expanded the authorities of U.S. law enforcement agencies to search telephone, email, medical, and financial records, and it also eased the restrictions on foreign intelligence gathering within the United States for the purpose of fighting terrorism."[4] The term "sanctuary" becomes a vague term that indicates a space, be it legal, virtual, or real, removed from the control of the state. Therefore, it is not only unacceptable but also incompatible with state grammar. It is in this sense that the term "insurgent sanctuaries" must be read, despite the

assumption that the text uses it to describe an insurgent system that gives protection and support to rebels and insurgents. It is in this latter framework that
"deportation to torture" emerges as justified and terms such as "immigrant" or
"alien" and "terrorist" tend to overlap as a potential "national security threat."[5]

Even at the beginning of European modernity, an act of Charles II defined
sanctuaries as "scandalous practices" that obstruct "the execution of legal processes."[6] Sanctuaries are an institution dating back to the Middle Ages, or even
further, to the Roman and Greek world. If sanctuaries gave protection not only to
criminals but also to serfs, excommunicates, heretics, "Jews, traitors, and others,
as well as to debtors and thieves,"[7] one should not intend this protection as if
it arose out of the benevolence of the church in times dominated by violence
and vengeance, the way the "Dark Ages" are usually portrayed. Sanctuaries, in
the Middle Ages, constituted an authoritative, legal sphere guaranteed by the
church and independent of the power of the king and other officers of the law.
The tension between sanctuaries and state, which would lead to their destruction as autonomous institutions, was not so much a clash between powers, that
of the church and that of the crown, as it was another example of a clash between
incompatible legal systems. On the one hand, a system based on obligations
and a plurality of autonomous authorities; on the other, a system that tended to
concentrate and monopolize power and give priority to rights over obligations.

The war between these legal systems is long and intense. In the sixteenth century, under the blows of the Reformation and a new configuration of state power,
the privileges or benefits of sanctuary were limited and abolished in the event of
treason. Henry VIII claimed the absolute prerogative to pardon. But in this war,
there were districts in London, as is the case of Whitefriars, or Alsatia, that were
able to extend the privilege of sanctuaries and immunity from civil process until
the end of the seventeenth century, when Charles II in 1697 put an end to any
immunity and dispersed the Alsatians.[8] This and other similar cases show that
the clash was not simply between church and state, clerical and lay apologists.
Reading the clash in these terms means ordering the historical material in the
light of the modern outcome of secularization.

The existence of the sanctuaries was also based on the involvement of neighborhoods and the collective behavior of local communities.[9] This third dimension, in addition to the relationship between church and crown, is essential in
understanding not only the dynamics of the latter relationship but especially the
functioning of a legal system based on customs, traditions, and habits—a system in which customs and traditions constitute a source of authority. It is from
this perspective that the tradition of sanctuaries transcends European borders.

Surprising new analogies, all to be investigated, can be found in the customary practices of Islamic countries and indigenous traditions.[10]

Historians often refer to the "abuse" of sanctuaries, in that they are a place of refuge for criminals of all sorts. Hence, their abolition would derive from the will to put an end to such abuse, from state regulation of punishment, and from the end of the violence typical of the Middle Ages.[11] This is a typical modern projection resulting from the unilinear conception of history characterized by the progress of juridical civilization that puts an end to abuses and the plurality of authority in the name of the state monopoly on violence (and abuses). The question to be investigated in this chapter concerns the contemporary existence of sanctuaries not as places of benevolence but as institutions characterized by a nonstate legality: not as places where an abstract right of immigrants is defended but as practices articulated around nonstate obligations and traditions, not as places where the protection of the church or other institutions is abused but as places where justice is implemented as a practical-political dimension and not a state-procedural one.

* * *

The sanctuary movement reached a certain degree of popularity in the United States when, in the 1980s, President Ronald Reagan began deporting refugees to their countries of origin. More than five hundred churches (and not only Christian churches) established themselves as sanctuaries for political asylum. From the 1980s to the present, this movement has continued its work, often away from the media's spotlight and the attention of political groups. In the United States, the sanctuary movement has once again received attention given Donald Trump's anti-immigrant policies. In Italy, the mayors of some cities decided not to apply the restrictive legal provisions required by the decree on security and immigration of 2018 drafted by Minister Salvini. Similar phenomena were taking place in Belgium, France, Germany, Greece, Poland, and other states.

Jürgen Quantz, pastor at the Heilig-Kreuz-Kirche in Berlin and founder of the German movement BAG Asyl in der Kirche, in an interview in November 2016 recounted his experience with migrants, who told him what he had to do.

They asked us what can we do? I was a priest here since 1980. They asked, Can't you help us? I said, Yes, what should we do? They said, You have an old right—asylum in the church. It is from the medieval period. In the Bible you can find stories—come into the sanctuary. This is your tradition, you should do it. I initially said No. I said, Here we have modern laws and rights. But they said, We think you should. I said Okay, I'll discuss it with my members of council. I lived with my family here—one night they knocked. I opened the door and the young people came and said it had to happen now. So I let them in.[12]

The reference is to a tradition common to Christians and Jews. It has its roots in Numbers 35:6–34: "Six of the towns you give the Levites will be cities of refuge, to which a person who has killed someone may flee. In addition, give them forty-two other towns. . . . They will be places of refuge from the avenger, so that anyone accused of murder may not die before they stand trial before the assembly." And it is taken up in Matthew 25:35: "I was a stranger and you invited me in." John T. Noonan, who worked as a US federal judge, rightly observed: "Sanctuary is shocking to the secular mind. How can there be any place within the confines of a nation that the law does not operate? How can religion claim a privilege to say it is beyond the law? How can the law stultify itself by acknowledging that in certain places the law ceases to hold sway?"[13]

If it is possible to answer these questions on a moral level by referring to a Christian sense, often forgotten today, of welcome and brotherhood, it remains to clarify the legality that has been shaped by sanctuary practices. It is the same legality that operated when churches were used as safe places for the enslaved who had escaped from their masters, the same legality that operates when immigrants are welcomed as brothers and sisters. From the point of view of this legality, the enslaved were not fugitive property and immigrants are not illegal aliens.[14] As already seen in previous chapters, the grammar of property and that of the modern nation-state were born together and mirror each other. The absolute and exclusive right of private property is the depoliticized side of the absolute right and power of the state to exclude human beings defined as aliens from the national territory. The former can extend to the right to kill a thief; the latter works daily by causing a number of immigrants to die at sea, on the borders, or in some detention center.[15] The Lockean right to kill a thief operates as the other side of the sovereign right to kill (or to let die) an alien. A logic that today is less and less rare to see in action. Today's law officials, who arrest, detain, deport immigrants and refugees, and feel authorized and justified in their actions as they operate under existing legislation should be reminded that Adolf Eichmann also believed that he was operating under existing law when he organized the deportation and massacre of the Jews. Eichmann presented himself as a mere official carrying out orders: "I was not a responsible leader, and as such do not feel myself guilty."[16] Immigration detention centers and border security centers are populated by little Eichmanns.

Now, the real issue is to provide theoretical and practical resources to question the rightness of the law. This means, from a theoretical point of view, dismantling the legal edifice on which the modern state and its monopoly of power are founded; from a practical point of view, it means investigating the legality configured in the practice of sanctuaries, in their reference to tradition and to a justice that goes beyond that of state procedures. As has been observed, "The sanctuary movement also presents a significant challenge to the assumption that government is sovereign regarding immigration policy."[17] The government remains sovereign, but the sanctuaries operate on the basis of an authority that is not derived or recognized by the state. This creates some confusion because a tension arises between the state monopoly over the power to exclude or include and a plurality of authorities that instead dilutes and disperses that power. This tension must be understood as one of the many symptoms of the decline of the nation-state and its monopoly on power. This tension can be described in terms of divergent moral principles and legitimacy, so that "communitarian values deprive administrative deportation efforts of the moral legitimacy that the classical order managed to sustain for so long."[18] However, the collapse of immigration enforcement is not produced by claims of a universal moral community but from much harsher processes of economic, political, and climatic globalization that make the nation-state obsolete as an instrument of regulation and synchronization. The decomposition of the state shows itself with different, antithetical aspects. On the one hand, we see the already obsolete attempt to reconfigure politics, citizenship, and democracy in cosmopolitan terms. On the other hand, we see the attempt to reconsolidate the sovereignty of the nation-state in terms of pervasive control over society and every sphere of individual action, especially including strengthening borders and intensifying the principle of exclusion on which to cement an already crumbling civil society. In the midst of these opposite but both markedly visible ways of managing decomposition, a plurality of morbid phenomena also proliferates. These are mostly deadly, but they are also a sign of the need for something different that is struggling to make its way. The alternative is not between an authoritarian nation-state and an unrealistic cosmopolitan democracy. It is not even between morality and politics. A different political grammar is needed. In the words of Jim Corbett, a celebrated activist of the sanctuary movement: "Individuals can resist injustice, but only communities can choose to do justice."[19] This difference is crucial for understanding the regime of legality of the sanctuaries, their incompatibility with respect to the grammar of the state, and the political possibilities they contain. It is not a question of resisting or disobeying unjust laws but of implementing institutions capable of giving rise to a more just order and a different regime of legality.

Citizenship is a status privilege based on the accidentality of place of birth or blood. It is the last fundament of the "right to have rights," without which the individual is dispossessed of membership in a community and the ability to act publicly and politically.[20] This privilege continues to exclude millions of individuals from a life of dignity. By juxtaposing citizens and aliens, the former term functions as the kind of "psychological wage" discussed by Du Bois in *Black Reconstruction*.[21] Not only are undocumented aliens forced to hold inferior jobs at low wages and without adequate social and health protections, but the "psychological wage" operates for citizens who, in exchange for the privilege of waving a national flag and the right to obtain a passport they will never use, accept little or no political participation and the benefits of property rights—even though they own nothing but their own labor power.

Alternative trajectories can and should emerge. Undocumented migrants go to school, work, and contribute to the reproduction of the community in which they live. As members of a community, they act in accordance with certain interpersonal obligations. Hence, the argument about rights and citizenship must be reversed. Citizenship is not a right but a practice.[22] It is not granted but exercised in a multiplicity of practices and obligations that constitute the true nature of the social fabric. These obligations are not reducible to the individual's obligation to obey the civil authority to which each person is presumed to have given consent. Rather, as Carole Pateman argues, "the members of the community are citizens in many political associations, which are bound together through horizontal and multifaceted ties of self-assumed political obligation." The political sphere is "the area of social existence in which citizens voluntarily cooperate together and sustain their common life and common undertaking."[23]

Obligations result from social practices that shape, produce, and reproduce common institutions. We always live within social and political bonds, as the theory of institutions has long shown. Santi Romano observed that even a criminal institution is an institution on a par with a school or a tennis club. Both require a form of legality and mutual obligations in order to continue to exist. In both cases, members have to behave in certain ways in order to remain members. A "revolutionary society or a criminal association does not constitute law from the viewpoint of the State that they try to subvert, or whose laws they violate, just as a schismatic sect is considered antilegalistic by the Church; but this does not imply that in the above case there are not institutions, organizations, and orders which, taken per se and intrinsically considered, are legal."[24]

It would be easy and wrong to understand the practice of sanctuaries as complementary to neoliberal policies that operate on the basis of exclusionary criteria distinguishing between migrants who are legal or illegal and those who are worthy of being helped or not. In such a conception, sanctuaries take the place of the state in providing care and making distinctions between worthy and unworthy migrants.[25] However, these perspectives—sanctuaries as moral shelters or appendages of neoliberal governmentality—are locked in a binary opposition between morals and politics, and are both inadequate to explore the field of possibilities that sanctuary practice can disclose. Nevertheless, even if sanctuary comes with risks of being a new kind of containment and refuge at the host's discretion, sanctuary practices should be understood in their own terms, as forms of legality independent from the state. Sanctuaries are neither solely about serving "victims," nor are they instances of mere opposition to state anti-immigration policies.

* * *

Let's go back to Pastor Jürgen Quantz, who began the sanctuary movement in Germany in 1983. There are some points in the interview he gave that are worth examining more closely. The first concerns the *ancient right of asylum,* which refers to the *medieval tradition* of sanctuaries. Another interesting element is the *tension between that tradition and modern laws and rights,* a tension that initially led Pastor Quantz to say no. But the migrants, and this is a third noteworthy point, replied that it was "his" tradition, the *tradition of the church* as an alternative to that of the law of the modern state. Again in Germany, a pastor engaged in the sanctuary movement declared that "the Bible is full of stories of refugees. . . . The passage from Exodus in the Old Testament was transposed to our community—'because you were strangers in the land of Egypt.'"[26] He is echoed by another pastor who claims to have practiced sanctuary "not from the so-called 'neighbourly love,' but from such recognition, as it is said in the Old Testament, 'Because you were strangers.'"[27] The reference to the tradition of the First Testament is important because it is the text shared by Judaism, Christianity, and Islam. But it should also be emphasized that this reference does not serve to locate the practice of sanctuaries entirely in religion; it is rather a call to an authority other than that of the state. An authority, one could say, far more ancient and universal than that of the nation-state.

If we want to grasp the element of novelty in the practice of sanctuaries, we must pay attention to the placement of this experience beyond the binary opposition of religion/secularism. This is an important displacement, especially since secularism has become a force for exclusion, a sort of secular religion, as, for example, in France, where *laïcité* has become a political weapon used by the right and the left against Muslim migrants.[28] Secularism is not about state neutrality; instead, it is a political device of neutralization, a political weapon, and a source of new conflict. The secular/religious binary has, since its inception, been configured as a device for controlling time and temporalization. The secular operated against the vertical temporality characterized by transcendence. It was the reference to this vertical dimension that made it possible to consider the existing order as inadequate, unjust, and thus to intervene practically to modify it. For this reason, in the Middle Ages, the protests of the oppressed took the form of protests against the control of time by the church. Apocalyptic expectations of an imminent end of time and the world were political ways of countering the justification of an earthly order. To assert itself, modern sovereignty has gone to war against this transcendent verticality, which is incorporated in the theological-political core of the state celebrated by Schmitt. The state has neutralized the public-political value of religion by relegating it to the private sphere of individual conscience; it has eradicated all claims of orientation toward a just transcendent order by sublating it into the authority of the law celebrated by Hobbes: *auctoritas non veritas facit legem*; it has attacked the social control of time exercised by the church and taken over its command. From here it emerges that the religious/secular binary has operated and operates as a mechanism that neutralizes attempts to question the existing order by referring to another temporality or to a superior idea of justice. It remains possible to challenge the law, but this can only be done in the private sphere and from opinions that the state may or may not *tolerate*. In this way, the secular/religious binary is juxtaposed with that of public/private. These and other binaries have the function of giving stability to the new political order of the sovereign state.

When Pastor Quantz points to the incommensurability between the ancient right of asylum and modern law, what emerges is a tension between different legal trajectories and temporal layers. This tension opens up unprecedented political possibilities in which the anachronistic medieval tradition of sanctuaries presents itself not as a rigid repetition of the past but as something dynamic and capable of new configurations that go beyond the secular/religious pairing. This reactivation of the medieval tradition of sanctuaries encloses a rich field of experimentation with institutional forms and nonstate authorities. But to grasp

this field of possibilities it is necessary, first of all, to free oneself from the teleological conception of history according to which the Middle Ages represents the
premodern—a dark era finally overcome by modernity. Teleology is a normative
view of history that, ex post, traces a progressive line in which *nonmodern* political, economic, and juridical configurations are defined as *premodern*, worthy
of being abandoned and overcome. If they survive in modernity, it is only as
remnants and delays. When we abandon this teleological conception of history,
however, the Middle Ages and the tradition of sanctuary appear as a rich arsenal
of juridical and political forms, with possibilities left unexplored or repressed.
Abandoning that teleological vision, the Middle Ages do not find a necessary outcome in capitalist and state modernity but appear as an arsenal of possibilities,
a clump of roads not taken and historical layers that continue to run alongside
the dominant trajectory of Western modernity. The tradition of sanctuaries is
one of these layers. If we can speak of the practice and tradition of sanctuaries as
anachronism, it is in the sense of a temporal friction between different historical
layers. Not an opposition, but as a field of possibilities.

The point is to avoid the dead end of the contrast between the law of the
church and that of the state and instead to direct one's sights and practice toward
other possibilities. These possibilities are constantly hidden by the juridical
mechanism of the modern state and by the synchronization of each institution
to its temporality.

* * *

"Within a country's borders there should be no place which is outside the law.
Its power should follow every citizen like a shadow. . . . To increase the number
of asylums is to create so many little sovereign states, because where the laws do
not run, there new laws can be framed opposed to the common ones and there
can arise a spirit opposed to that of the whole body of society. The whole of history shows that great revolutions, both in states and in the views of men, have
issued forth from places of asylum."[29] Beccaria's discourse has fascinated liberals,
who typically see only one side of his claim for unitary sovereignty, i.e., that no
one be outside the law or above the law. What liberals do not see and do not
want to see is that it is in the nature of the state to constantly expand its control
over society or, in Beccaria's words, to "follow every citizen like a shadow."[30]

Beccaria's discourse against asylum (sanctuaries) is symptomatic of a way of
understanding the relationship between state power and the rights of the individual. Beccaria's name is commonly associated with the criticism of torture in

the name of the defense of individual rights as the basis of the legitimacy of the state. The crucial issue is that the "progressive" side of Beccaria's discourse on individual rights is made one with his critique of asylum, which, by shattering sovereignty, would constitute an attack against the dogma of the unity of the nation-state, the monopoly of state power, the depoliticization of the social. It is a typically liberal way of understanding the relationship between freedom and power: The former is individual, the latter monopolized by the state. Dominant political modernity is characterized by an enormous process of singularization and synchronization in which the different *libertates* of groups are atomized into the singular freedom of the individual; the numerous corporative and collective *auctoritates* are shattered and subsumed in the state monopoly of power. In historical terms, this is the process of the original accumulation of political power, a process that has been articulated through numerous demarcations and binaries.

Beccaria's enlightenment expresses a way of understanding the relationship between society and state totally befitting this process: Starting here, sovereignty is concentrated in the hands of the state, and society is individualized and deprived of political power. State power finds no real counterpower existing within society but, according to what will become a liberal dogma, limits itself through procedural and constitutional mechanisms of the rule of law. But the history of the last two and a half centuries has repeatedly shown that the limit that power places on itself can be continually redefined or even suspended in the name of real or presumed emergencies. This is what happens repeatedly in many states today: From the state's point of view, migrants constitute an emergency or a danger against which physical walls and legal barriers are built. A number of aliens may descend into the shadowy realm of the outlaw. Some states transition to authoritarian rule without a formal breach of their constitutional order. Almost everywhere, executive power bullies the other powers and takes the place to which the legislative body is rightfully entitled. The current situation shows the bankruptcy of a worn-out regulatory package built on a vaguely liberal-democratic conception of the state. It is not a question of issuing an updated normative package from above. Rather, it is a matter of extracting a sort of exemplary normativity from contemporary events—a normativity that takes shape in the practices and risks of politics. It is with this perspective that, in these pages, we should look at sanctuaries.

This is the voice of the state against sanctuary activists: "If this Government is going to represent *all the people of this nation*, it cannot favor those which commit criminal acts and contend that they are immune from prosecution, because they are motivated by a *higher authority*."[31] Beccaria and his liberal followers, including the attorney prosecuting the Tucson activists, subscribe to the same discourse: "Within a country's borders there should be no place which is outside the law."[32] Sovereignty is one and indivisible. If this is the case, then from the point of view of the state, something that is far more subversive than giving shelter to undocumented migrants lurks around the term "sanctuaries" and their tradition. From the point of view of the state, religious freedom is a private freedom and must remain so. Religious freedom is guaranteed within the category of fundamental rights, and cults can freely proliferate only in the private sphere of individual liberties. Sanctuaries, be they churches, practice, or tradition, go beyond the private sphere in which the modern state has confined religion and claim an authority that, from the point of view of the state, they should not have. The prosecutor, in order to deny any reference to a "higher authority," unwittingly put himself in a difficult position when he "told jurors that there was nothing in the Bible that told believers to break the law."[33] In this way the prosecutor affirmed the state monopoly of the exact interpretation of the Bible, and, to demarcate the separation between church and state, he himself violated that separation, transforming the state into a theologian. The practice of sanctuaries, their reference to a "higher authority," had rendered that demarcation fluid, together with that of public and private, legal and illegal. Let's see what this opposition consists of.

In one of the last chapters of *Discipline and Punish*, Michel Foucault deals with the relationship between illegalities and delinquency. With the notion of illegalism, Foucault wants to highlight the multiple practices of differentiation, categorization, hierarchization, and social management of behaviors defined as undisciplined.[34] The penalty here is represented as a way of dealing with illegalities that often intersect with social conflicts and struggles against political regimes. Mainly interested in the production of the criteria of exclusion, discipline, and transformation of illegalism (*illégalisme*) into delinquency, Foucault characterizes illegalism in oppositional terms, such as French peasants' *refusal* to pay taxes, *refusal* of conscription, or *refusal* of a new proprietary regime. It is about "illegal practices" *against* the "law itself and the justice whose task it was to apply it; *against* local landowners who introduced new rights; *against* employers who worked together, but forbade workers' coalitions; *against* entrepreneurs who introduced more machines."[35] In essence, according to Foucault, it is *against* the new forms of law and the rigors of regulations, as well as *against* the new regime of land ownership and legal exploitation of labor, that the opportunities for infractions multiply and illegalities develop. Foucault's remarkable contribution lies in having shown how the penal system, imposed beginning in the eighteenth century and affirmed by the French Revolution, tends not merely to repress illegalisms but rather to differentiate them. Foucault traces this history by analyzing the legal categories and institutions designed to control and sanction illegalism.

But the category has a limit. It takes shape and makes sense only when a multiplicity of practices is subsumed in what is prescribed or forbidden by the legal code, that is, when the code system has already replaced another legality, such as a preexisting common law. From the point of view of those who practice common law, not only is there no illegalism, but the category of resistance is also inadequate. These are not individuals who act against the new forms of law and the rigors of regulations but rather communities that operate under a different legal regime. The clash is between two legal orders or, in other words, between two or more distinct political and juridical temporalities in conflict with one another. I use the term temporalities to highlight the tension between different historical trajectories—one that presents itself as progressive and another that is cast as outdated or anachronistic. This clash has happened repeatedly during the nineteenth century in France, the twentieth century in Russia, and today in Chiapas, Mexico, and Bolivia. Those who *disobey* the legal regime of modern property relations do so not simply against it but because they *obey* a different order of duties and rights, an order based on different customs and traditions.

History written by Foucault, however brilliant, is a history written from the point of view of the new legal order that recodes, disciplines, and controls practices that the order itself defines as illicit but that for a long time coexisted alongside the code not as illegalisms but as customs, traditions, and different legal systems. What interests Foucault is how these practices are punished; their tradition and autonomous life interest him less. For Foucault, at least in *Discipline and Punish*, they become objects of interest only when they are already caged in the new legal system, which encodes them in terms of illegalism.

However, things appear differently as soon as we consider the practice of sanctuaries in light of traditions and customs that have an autonomous life, independent of the grasp of penal institutions and the state. They constitute an anachronism open to innovative political outcomes. If state rationality tends to synchronize them until they become either its appendices or forms of illegalism, the challenge begins when this binary logic is called into question. From the point of view of the state, when nonlegal practices are inscribed in a binary code that recodes them as illegal, there may be removals, resistances, and conflicts but not real alternatives, which instead may emerge when a different authority is evoked. This is what the migrants remind Pastor Jürgen Quantz of. Instead of opposition or disobedience to state laws, a friction takes place between political temporalities and trajectories characterized by different, incommensurable juridical grammars.

It can be instructive to see the encounter/clash of these distinct grammars in a courtroom. Here are the facts: In the 1980s, in the United States, activists of the sanctuary movement organized a network of congregations that, proclaiming themselves to be sanctuaries, hosted undocumented migrants from Central America. In doing so they violated the existing legislation on asylum and immigration rights. From the point of view of the state, these were illegal practices. The activists were accused of plotting against the US government, and the sentences reached up to five years in prison and various fines. The state's response, according to the prosecutor, was that a country, as sovereign, "has the absolute power to control their borders";[36] that only the state has the authority to apply the law and the responsibility to punish criminals; that private citizens, in this case activists, have no right to host "undocumented migrants" and, even less, the authority to determine the legal status of immigrants.

This was the outcome of the trial—unexceptional, from the point of view of state legality. But if we rewind the tape, we can review the facts from the point of view of the Tucson activists. They defined their practice as a "civil initiative," emphasizing that it was not "civil disobedience."[37] This distinction was not just terminology or a legal ploy to avoid tougher penalties. For the activists it was not a question of disobeying unjust laws but of giving effectiveness to just laws that the government was ignoring. In other words, the words of the activists, *civil initiative*, unlike civil disobedience, become law by practicing natural rights.[38] *Civil initiative* is neither resistance to injustice nor a petition for justice to be done: "*Civil initiative* means doing justice."[39] It is a practice based on the "powers of the community rather than the government."[40] In this regard, the civil initiative forecasts a third possible political trajectory beyond the dichotomy of legality/illegality.

Two different legal grammars were facing each other. The state coherently expressed its own point of view. The public prosecution reaffirmed the monopoly of state power to determine and control the borders, to punish illegalisms, and to repress the attempt by private subjects to claim for themselves some authority not granted and legitimized by the state. In other words, the state reiterated its binary grammar based on the private/public, legal/illegal, citizen/alien, and friend/enemy pairings. Reaffirming, as the prosecution did, that the activists were *private* citizens and therefore lacking the authority to act as they had meant, on the one hand, redefining their activity as *illegal* and, on the other, accusing them of having challenged the monopoly of state power. The state could, at best, understand the language of *civil disobedience*, but it could not, in any way, recognize in the practice of the activists any kind of *legal activity*. The binary logic of state legality had been challenged by a third political practice, one beyond the dualism of obedience/disobedience. Referring to their own practice in terms of *legal activity*, the Tucson activists implicitly referred to another legal discourse and to another authority: the *authority* to intervene in the legal field of asylum law and immigration legislation. In essence, by making their position toward the state even more difficult, they claimed a different authority as the source of legitimization for their *legal practice*. Along with the medieval tradition of sanctuaries, there is the tradition of natural rights that emerges in the practices and discourses of the activists.

* * *

"We believe Sanctuary is a vision continuously created through decades of struggle, through thousands of years of struggle." Thus, begins the *Statement on Sanctuary* published in 2017 by the New Sanctuary Movement of Philadelphia.[41] This sentence is important because it recalls, on the one hand, a tradition of sanctuaries that dates back thousands of years and, on the other, a history of struggles that from time to time redefined the political space of the sanctuary. It is not a static, museum tradition but a living tradition articulated through conflicts that keeps the space of democracy open. Because this is precisely what is at stake: the inseparability between conflict and democratic practice. In this connection, the sanctuary takes shape as "a vision": "We are working, organizing, reaching and yearning towards that vision—a vision of collective and personal transformation." Where democracy is actually experienced, a political miracle that fuses individual and collective transformation takes place. This is an ancient political position that poses the question of change as a primary issue of politics. In Western history, this question was at the center of Plato's politics: If the just order of the polis is one in which just rulers govern, only a polis already governed by just rulers can produce just citizens who are also able to govern according to justice. The miracle that breaks this circle is, then, the Republic: not a utopia to bring about but a dialectic between the soul and the order of the polis.[42] The miracle is not an external intervention that comes to the aid of philosophy; rather, it is characterized by a relation with the divine, which is the relation to the idea of good and justice. In Plato's terms, the philosopher "consorting with what is ordered and divine . . . himself becomes as ordered and divine as a human being can."[43]

This participation in the idea transforms both the nature of philosophy and political practice, on the one side and, on the other, the philosophers and rulers, who, by participating in it, become themselves well ordered and divine. The philosopher, who is not "a pure theorist unable to touch any practical task,"[44] in the practice of the dialogue takes responsibility for his own soul, urging his interlocutors to do the same. It is in this spirit that Plato goes to Syracuse: to urge Diogenes to be in harmony with himself, because only they who are just can govern with justice. The same issue extends across thousands of years of history. It emerges in Kant's concern about the impossibility of constructing the optimal city if, first, the people who must construct it do not improve themselves; it is at the heart of Marx's third thesis on Feuerbach, when he defines revolutionary practice as "the coincidence of the changing of circumstances and of human activity or self-changing." We have seen it in the practice of the Diggers, in the mystic practice of the *Entwerden* revived by Müntzer, and in many other social practices.

It reemerges in the sanctuary movements. Ontario Sanctuary Coalition activists, in contact with those in Tucson, have gone so far as to define their practice as "a state within the state," questioning the state monopoly of power and acting as a public authority.[45] It should be emphasized here that the term "state" in that phrase has two very different meanings. Indeed, the practice of *civil initiative* does not reproduce the state but brings out a political and legal practice in which the constitutive barriers of modern political configuration, such as inclusion and exclusion, friends and enemies, citizens and aliens, are eroded together with the separation between spiritual and temporal. The spiritual dimension acts as a bond (*religio*), as a link based on the practices that define the space-time of the sanctuary. These practices are directed neither against the state nor to make the state do something for migrants. Rather, they are guided by an idea of justice that goes beyond the state, its borders, and grammar. The idea of brotherhood, which from biblical texts goes on to constitute the incandescent core of natural rights in the French Revolution and the Declaration of the Rights of Man and of the Citizen, is here reactivated to merge the particular and the universal in the practice of sanctuaries. This convergence cannot be built in the laboratories of political theory. It is not a utopia to realize. It is real in the practice of brotherhood, whose temporality is the now-time.

The notion of brotherhood should not be channeled solely into the small-minded trajectory of nationalism, as has often been done by modern political theory. The nation-state was only one of the possible outcomes of the Revolution. And it was an outcome that established itself by blocking, with exceptional state violence, other possible trajectories. However, these other trajectories have not disappeared without leaving traces. The call to brotherhood formed the emblem of the workers' movement in 1848, in 1871, and in numerous other events. It reemerges in the movement of sanctuaries because if human beings are brothers, the fundamental political question is not, in a Schmittian way, to divide them up as either friends or enemies. One can choose friends but *not* brothers and sisters.[46] With brothers and sisters, we must learn not only to live together, but we must also create the conditions for living together in justice. Sanctuaries as institutions rooted in the social fabric welcome anyone in need of protection, not only from a foreign government but also from a domestic one. This welcome, like the love of which Paul speaks in Romans 13:8—"For the one who loves another has fulfilled the law"—is not directed toward the neighbor or those with whom we have chosen to live in community but toward the other (ἕτερον) whom we have not chosen.

Disagreement and conflict are always possible—we only need to learn how to handle them in a mature way. This is perhaps the most important task of sanctuaries as practice: the coincidence between changes in external circumstances and human activity as self-education for self-transformation. In the practice of sanctuaries, activists and refugees test new forms of social bonds and subjectivation. The refugees are not victims here, passive and vulnerable, but common brothers, sisters, and actors in experiments in which the state is kept at a distance. It is not a matter of opposing the state or violating its laws. These behaviors are not only already included in the logic of the state, but they also legitimize its existence. The alternative to the state can be found in legal traditions to be restored—traditions that flow through unsynchronized layers of time. If the paradigms of resistance, revolution, and disobedience are still determined by their subordination to the grammar of the state, *civil initiative* is an experiment that tries to speak, perhaps still hesitantly, a different language.[47] We must, modestly, try to extract new legal and political concepts from this language.

* * *

"Now if in the Middle Ages churches could offer sanctuary to the most common of criminals, could they not do the same today for the most conscientious among us? And if in the Middle Ages they could offer forty days to a man who had committed a sin and a crime, could they not today offer an indefinite period to one who had committed no sin?"[48] In these terms, in 1966, the Reverend William Sloane Coffin Jr. revitalized the tradition of sanctuaries to give hospitality to young people who refused to go to war in Vietnam. For his actions, the Reverend Coffin was arrested and convicted of conspiring against the United States.

In an essay on the notion of authority, Myriam Revault d'Allones showed that if space is the matrix of power, in the sense that power determines boundaries and exclusions, time is the matrix of authority, in the sense that it concerns the link between the past and the present, the tension between continuity and discontinuity.[49] Power, one could add, is leaning to break that link. The idea of revolution as a *novus ordo seclorum* emphasizes the break with the past, not unlike the political theory developed by Hobbes and Locke when they erase preexisting theoretical traditions and imagine the construction ex nihilo of the political order. Modern power is configured as sovereignty on borders but also as a dominion over historical time: on a present to be controlled, a future to be oriented, a past to be rendered inert, usually by enclosing it within the confines of a museum. For the state, the past exists as a narrative to be invented for the use and consumption of the present and in the interest of national history. Whatever is not functional to this synchronization of historical time can easily be branded as a relic or anachronism.

However, anachronism also works in different ways. The anachronism of sanctuaries, their reference to the Middle Ages and to an even older tradition, serves as an anticipation of new political configurations. The reference to the medieval tradition of sanctuaries is not romantic; it is anachronistic in the sense that it interrupts the temporality of the state and opens up a field of possibilities for new juridical and political configurations. In this sense, the Middle Ages appear as an enormous arsenal of *nonmodern* juridical, economic, and political concepts and practices. The tradition of sanctuaries, far older than Christianity, reemerged in the Middle Ages. In the thirteenth century, the number of sanctuary churches in England and northern France exceeded thirty thousand.[50] The end of this tradition retrospectively illuminates the sense of the practice of sanctuaries. Well before Beccaria's Enlightenment, in the sixteenth century the attack on sanctuaries took place in the clash between the plurality of coexisting authorities and legal systems and the (proto)modern sovereign attempt to impose a new homogeneous and synchronized territorial space together with a new conception of punishment. This attack, in the sixteenth century, saw the nascent sovereign state and Lutheranism as allies. The Reformation broke the ties with the authority of Rome and created space for a reconfiguration of the monarchy as supreme authority. At the same time, cases of violation of sanctuaries by the king increased, especially when protection was given to political enemies or rebels. In England, in 1534–1536, "all persons accused or suspected of high treason were debarred from the privilege or benefit of sanctuary."[51] During the reign of Henry VIII, the 1540 act mandated that "sanctuary and abjuration no longer apply to a number of high felonies."[52] The *abjuratio regni* was a "combination of voluntary exile and banishment"[53] and worked as a mechanism to solve tensions by allowing one party in a dispute to remove oneself, either permanently or for a certain time, from the jurisdiction of a specific authority. Through subsequent legislative acts, Henry VIII eliminated these mechanisms of conflict mediation by placing the monopoly of punishment, mercy, and pardon in the hands of the crown and removing this prerogative from other authorities, be they local or the church. In this battle between legal systems, the crown sought to appropriate the total right to punish and pardon. The crime was configured as an attack on public order, and the distinction between sin and crime was no longer related to different and even competing legal competences. Now the former fell within the internal forum of the individual, while the latter was the exclusive jurisdiction of the external legal forum.[54] This distinction was formalized in Hobbes's political theory.

The long war between legal orders included and at the same time exceeded the religious clash. Mary Tudor did little or nothing to restore the privilege of sanctuaries. In 1624, James I won a new battle in the war between legal systems by declaring that "no sanctuary or privilege of sanctuary should thereafter be admitted or allowed in any case."[55] The trajectory of the nascent modern state, that is, the concentration of power against other authorities, and the trajectory of the nascent capitalist mode of production intertwined during the seventeenth century: An act of 1697 by the Whig-dominated Parliament put an end to sanctuary for debtors.[56]

These acts against sanctuaries were also acts against the legal autonomy of neighborhoods and communities that often reacted with riots to arrests by government officials. A large number of "rebellious riots and tumults" led to the Riot Act of 1715, which provided that if a tumultuous meeting of twelve or more people failed to disperse, offenders "shall be adjudged felons, and shall suffer death as in a case of felony without benefit of clergy."[57] It was not uncommon for the writ of habeas corpus to be suspended in the war against local authorities. The state of exception and the suspension of fundamental rights are not a recent invention of the state threatened by internal or external enemies but ordinary mechanisms of the birth and functioning of the state.

The war against local authorities and their self-defense must be seen in the right perspective. The revolts against imprisonment were not for the simple defense of criminals but to defend institutions, authorities, and an independent legal system, one incompatible with that of the modern state. What contemporaries and historians generally define as "abuses" committed by sanctuaries are "practices" incompatible with those of the nascent legal system. It is only in the conflict, and then only from the point of view of the dominant legal system, that such practices corresponding to a different legal system are qualified as "abuse." From this perspective, the war against the legal autonomy of sanctuaries was described in terms of a struggle against "quarters of London which were populated by the outcasts of society."[58] These neighborhoods were also described as "breeders of subversion and vice,"[59] "relics of the barbarism of the darkest ages" populated by knaves, libertines, and abandoned women.[60] Among these was the sanctuary of Whitefriars, known as Alsatia, which in addition to practicing certain measures of self-government continued to exercise the privilege of protecting debtors from arrest. These were districts removed from state law, regulated by local authorities and customary rights, and in which the "civil power was unable to keep order"[61]—that is, to impose the order of law and the state. This was the unacceptable abuse: not the absence of order but the absence of *state* order.

* * *

There existed a different system of legality that must be understood in terms of institutions that were autonomous from the state.[62] This alternative order to the state, according to the logic of internal colonialism, was described as "relics of the barbarism of the darkest ages."[63] The war against sanctuaries was part of an attack on areas capable of exercising jurisdictional immunities and was intertwined with a new mercantile regime. Hence the hostility toward the existence of spaces where debtors and vagabonds could find refuge. The destruction of the sanctuaries gave way to a new prison system and to workhouses. The "abjuration of the realm" ceased to be a mechanism of self-regulation of the conflict that "allowed an offender time to plead for pardon."[64] The punishment had to be swift and effective. The abjuration, once suppressed for numerous felonies in the 1540 act, was reconfigured by state power and turned into the power to transport convicts across the Atlantic and sell them as indentured servants.[65] A new penal practice more suitable to the state and the new private property regime was born.

Other legal and criminal systems were defeated. The question about the reason for that defeat is badly posed. Those systems were not defeated by "necessity" or by some Hegelian "cunning of reason." If there is no reversed teleology that legitimizes the victory of a certain state, penal, and proprietary order that has led to the present Western civilization, if one stops fantasizing about forms of transition from one system to another, condemning all that is barbaric and worthy of disappearing, if one stops reconstructing these transitions by projecting modern concepts onto the past, then a war between different systems emerges. One system is defeated by chance in the same way that another can impose itself by "luck." *Fortuna* and *virtù* are key categories of Machiavelli's conception of politics. What about "virtue"? Virtue consists in making new political forms emerge from the ruins of existing forms.[66] Alternatives are not to be invented out of thin air but taken from how today's practices reconfigure the past to create something different. To do this, it is necessary to dig into the historical material, to bring out real, otherwise unthinkable differences with respect to the dominant modernity.

The conception of punishment offers a privileged point of view for understanding the medieval practice of sanctuaries, but it must be looked at not only from the point of view of punishment but also from that of the regulation of conflict. Keep in mind that medieval English law was not worried about the fact that refugees in a sanctuary could avoid punishment.[67] In fact, the roots of the practice of sanctuaries are found in the practice of *intercessio*, which, in Roman society, corresponded to an institutional procedure of reciprocal limitation of powers and intervention of a third party in a dispute in order to avoid injustice.[68] In the late fourth century, this Romanist tradition intersected with the ecclesiastical tradition and was given over to the authority of the bishops. For a fixed period of time, generally forty days, the sanctuary churches housed subjects who had violated a law in order to reach an agreement between the parties and allow for reconciliation. It was a crucial institution in a society characterized by a plurality of authorities, where a wrongdoing, a reparation, or an act of revenge could easily give rise to a feud. Using and mixing different traditions, the medieval legal order had internally created an institution capable of preventing the escalation of conflicts through another way of understanding punishment and regulating conflicts. If the practice of sanctuaries was not widespread in Italy, one reason for its absence can be traced to the fact that the local governments, at least until the fourteenth century, had as their primary purpose reconciliation between the criminal and the victim, not the punishment of the offender.[69] In other words, sanctuaries were not present in Italy not because of the weakness of the church but because they were less necessary. Furthermore, Italy was characterized by a multiplicity of municipal institutions and city-states, which constituted an alternative both to sanctuaries and to the formation of a united kingdom.

From a modern Western point of view, it would be easy to highlight the instability of the medieval order, in which the plurality of authorities and legal systems, including sanctuaries, was always on the verge of producing conflicts and feuds. This is Beccaria's perspective. However, if we change our perspective, the practice of sanctuaries instead shows a way to deal with conflict in the presence of a plurality of authorities or, in modern terms, in the absence of the state monopoly of power. Against the modern paradigm of the neutralization of conflict through the singularization and monopolization of public power in the hands of the state, sanctuaries present a nonmodern alternative to the regulation of conflict, and not only because of the religious dimension to which they refer. The practice of sanctuaries should not be read through the moralizing lenses of the benevolence of the church, ready to give hospitality to criminals, but as the anomaly, in modern terms, of *intercessio*, of a suspension of space and sovereign time by means of another authority. It is this anomaly that lurks in the anachronism of the medieval tradition of sanctuary.

Anachrony, in political terms, is the gateway to *tertium datur*, the third possible way to interrupt the unilinear vision of historical time. As suggested earlier, what emerges from the practice of the sanctuary movement is something more profound than civil disobedience to laws judged morally unjust. It is a challenge to the binary logic of the state through the practice of an extrastate authority, which some activists named "civil initiative." If the activists define their practice as "legal activity," the question concerns the nature of the *authority* based on which their activity can be defined as legitimate within a legal regime that does not coincide with that of the state. We can begin to shed light on this authority, as a practice, if we abandon the vision of the vulnerability of refugees and migrants as victims. We need to look at the practice of sanctuaries not so much as places where one escapes *from* a danger but as places *to which* one runs to seek alternative human, social, and political relations.[70] These are institutions that, if placed outside the legality of the state, are at the same time characterized by their intrinsic legality. In fact, if one can speak of the legality of the practice of sanctuaries, as the Tucson activists have, it is pursuant to an authority that has a nonstate origin and that is not defined in opposition to the state but as another tradition and alternative political trajectory to that of the modern nation-state. These are archaic, or anachronistic, institutions that represent a "democratic counterthrust to statism."[71] In the reactivation of sanctuaries today, one can see not only the need to give hospitality to migrants but above all a need for democracy that exceeds not just this or that particular state law but the logic of the modern state as such—its monopoly of power and its binary logic built on exclusions and depoliticizations. Perhaps, in the crisis of the state and some of its fundamental categories, we are witnessing not only morbid phenomena of authoritarianism, renewed attacks on sanctuary, and new configurations of friends and enemies but also the emergence of new institutional forms that may outline a different order of the present. Sanctuary is a good concrete concept to rethink citizenship as performed citizenship. Renan's old description of the nation as a daily plebiscite must be overthrown in favor of more humble daily obligations performed in concrete institutions. The state does not disappear, but it is no longer the sovereign that decides on inclusion and exclusion. Instead, it becomes a service apparatus for the functioning of the democratic institutions that control it. The state does not decide who is entitled to health care and who is not; it simply provides adequate facilities. It does not decide who is entitled to education and who is not; it simply provides facilities in which education can take place. It does not decide who is a citizen and who is not; it simply provides means and facilities to facilitate practices of civil, political, and social citizenship. From being an end, the state becomes a means.

It is in this way that in the present situation, the practice of sanctuaries can be thought. To do this it is good to go back to the *Statement on Sanctuary* of 2017: "This disastrous political moment is also the birth of something big and beautiful and powerful. It is the birth of an expanded Sanctuary for everyone. . . . This is a vision defined and organized by undocumented people who have lived in the urgency all along. . . . This is the moment to build bridges with different communities and join forces. We see Sanctuary as the umbrella that covers all of us from the storm, and the womb to birth a new world. We are committed to the work of building not just a Sanctuary City, but a Sanctuary world."[72] Sanctuaries can constitute a virtuous anachronism that anticipates a different, nonstate, social way of being together. An alternative to the most arbitrary and enduring form of status privilege: that of national citizenship. The concept of citizenship constitutes the apex of the logic of the state, in which a multiplicity of oppositions converges and is reconfigured in the opposition between citizens and noncitizens as aliens. Here, in this status privilege that is citizenship, an enormous variety of degrees of exclusion from civil, political, and social rights is channeled.

AFTERWORD

The task of politics and theory today is to engage in the configuration of new concepts. These emerge when the structure of an entire legal edifice begins to crumble. Through the cracks gleams a new light. As Machiavelli would have put it, the decline of existing legal forms is our good fortune. But with decline also comes anxiety about the uncertain.

In the last three chapters of this book, I examined three pillars of the modern political form—property, political representation, and citizenship. I showed how the same logic of exclusion runs through them. Private property, configured as the exclusive ownership of a good, is historically characterized by the exclusion of forms of common possession that denote a different relationship to the world. Political representation, which emerged as a mechanism to make visible the unity of the sovereign people, is in fact what excludes them from political life and the most relevant decision-making processes. Its logic produces serial and depoliticized individuals and, at the same time, shatters existing political collectivities into individual atoms. But the demos is not easily anesthetized. Its presence goes beyond the representative mechanism. It is what I have called *democratic excess*.

Finally, citizenship is the political apex of a pyramid of exclusions that begins with civil and political rights and ends with the opposition between citizen and alien. It is in many ways the most brutal of exclusions, the ultimate status privilege that continues to exclude not only those without citizenship but especially those without citizenship considered "decent." The many migrants who would rather throw their papers overboard than meet the border police with the "wrong citizenship" understand this. The assumption in international law that nations are equal as sovereigns is and remains a fiction. You can experience this on a daily basis at any international airport, or, in a horrific form of Dante's *Inferno*, whenever migrants are left to die at sea or in a desert. While Dante's damned may have had sins to atone for, migrants are only guilty of being born in the "wrong" place and with the "wrong" citizenship.

These forms of exclusion cannot be eliminated through theory alone. It is not the idea of cosmopolitan democracy that will save the souls of migrant-aliens. Nor are there any theoretical recipes for solving the crisis of democracy and the growing mistrust of the masses toward the ruling elites. The nationalization of companies and giant corporations has proven to be nothing more than a shift of ownership from private to state hands, a shift that does not change the logic of property relations. In other words, the conceptual and theoretical arsenal available today is insufficient to overcome the current state of affairs. It is exhausted to the point that it is not even sufficient to understand our present. Often, it perpetuates the very evils it seeks to eliminate.

Hence the growing sense of being stuck in the present, with a future that takes the form of a climate apocalypse and a past that for some should be erased and for others is more attractive than both the present and the uncertain future. The inhabitants of the present operate without an adequate compass. Both orientation based on tradition and orientation based on the idea of progress have ceased to function. Thus, surrogate orientations emerge: Conservative forces refer to a fantasy of the past; so-called liberal and progressive forces orient themselves on the basis of moralizing categories to divide the world into good and evil, the righteous and the basket of deplorables.

The famous Kantian question of orientation returns as an unsolved problem of modernity: *How to orient oneself in thinking?* This problem arose with Cartesian metaphysics and, in politics, with the erasure of preexisting traditions and customs. The question today can be rephrased in these terms: How to orient oneself in our present? That is, in a present that has liquefied all foundations and transformed nature into language. The Cartesian ego has expanded to become the infinite free will that Hegel described as foundation of modern private property. The answer to the question of orientation does not come from theory or fiction. There are political practices, which I explore in the last three chapters of this book, that disarticulate and rearticulate the current legal, political, and economic material into new configurations. These practices are not definitive solutions to contemporary problems. They are experiments with the world and ourselves that help us better understand the meaning of these problems. These experiments should be seen as theory in action. This is the method behind *Revolution and Restoration*: to consider political practices and social movements as theory in action and sites of concept production.

In these practices, terms that are seen as anachronistic, unprogressive, or directly regressive can create tensions useful for concept configuration. This is the case with religious practices, customary traditions, and legal obligations. Today, the language of rights has expanded to invade every sphere of life and reality in general. Civilization has saturated the world with rights and laws. Its true colonial character is legal before cultural. It lies in the expansion of *civil* law. It is what Henry Sumner Maine defined as the movement of progressive societies, that is, the movement from status to contract. Today there are rights of animals, of plants, of lakes and mountains. There are the rights of those yet to be born, and there is the right to change the past.

The power of the legal lies in its artificiality. The law reifies human relationships by making them impersonal and by mediating conflicts through a third authority: the state. In today's upside-down world, natural rights have become the rights of nature. The former are claimed by conservative forces to legitimize property and traditional forms of marriage. The latter are waved as banners by so-called progressive forces, who applaud with satisfaction the inclusion of Mother Nature in state constitutions. Thus, in the name of universal protection, nature is reified as a subject of law, with the state as its guarantor. But precisely for this reason, the state that grants rights also retains the power to suspend them, to abolish them, and to make constant exceptions. The certain result of the inclusion of the protection of nature in the articles of a constitution is the neutralization of the political and legal authority of the communities that had previously taken care of it in a relationship unmediated by the state.

On the other hand, natural rights provided the revolutionary energy to overthrow injustice and inequality and gave the Diggers the legal tools to defend forms of common possession against modern dynamics of private appropriation. They constituted the language of obligations as a balance of individualized rights. It was on the basis of relations of obligation that, in natural law, the poor could take from the rich when they were in need. For the *ius naturale*, this act is not theft or sin. Rather, it is based on the obligation of the rich to share with the poor when the latter are in need. But instead of working from this natural law tradition and extending it to include the homeowner's obligation to allow the needy to use an unused dwelling, thereby finding a traditional basis for justifying the occupation of unused dwellings, the so-called left has ceded the natural law arsenal to the conservative forces. We must never forget that the political terms we use are battle terms. Their semantics are defined from time to time in concrete conflicts.

The language of obligation also emerges in the imperative mandate, according to which representatives have not only rights but primarily obligations to the communities and assemblies that have mandated them and that continue to retain the authority to control their actions, including the power of revocation. Again, it is the language of obligation that emerges in the practice of sanctuaries, where the appeal to biblical tradition and the obligation to provide refuge conflicts with the power of the state to decide who has the right to stay and who must be repatriated or locked up in some detention center.

In each of these practices, a specific tension between legal systems emerges: the tension between private property and practices of common ownership; the tension between representative democracy and the imperative mandate; and the tension between national citizenship and traditional practices of sanctuary, often rooted in religion and operating at the local level. These tensions are simultaneously characterized by asynchronous temporalities and clashes between mutually incompatible legal systems. Incompatibility means that national sovereignty, private property, and national citizenship are in constant conflict with traditional customs, premodern and religious institutions that are seen as vestiges of past eras or anachronisms. From the perspective of *Revolution and Restoration*, these institutions are indeed anachronisms that generate tensions with the progressive and synchronizing temporality of the state, but they are also fruitful anachronisms capable of generating concrete alternatives.

The tensions described transcend the specific form of modern sovereignty and are configured in terms that challenge the opposition of revolution and restoration, of present and past. This is made clear in the first chapter. The tension between past and present opened up by the reactivation of anachronistic elements, by their restoration, is not a return to the past. The very idea of a return to the past is impossible and presupposes a unilinear conception of historical time, like railroad tracks along which the train of history can reverse and return to the previous station. Or speed up to reach the next station more quickly. These two opposing conceptions, return and acceleration, reflect the Jacobin revolutionary conception and the reaction of the counterrevolutionaries. These conceptions mirror each other: In both cases, the locomotive of history is the state, this engineer of time, which has the power to control acceleration, modernization, progress, revolution, and counterrevolution. These attempts to control historical time have the same result: the sovereign dictatorship of the state. De Maistre and Robespierre are the two sides of the modern conception of sovereign power.

Revolution and Restoration works with and within tensions as they produce the energy needed to reconfigure institutions and legal structures. In the clash, nothing remains unchanged, neither the anachronistic structures that are reactivated nor the legal forms of the state that oppose them. The clash changes all terms. An appropriate method is needed to study the genesis of these changes and, with them, the genesis of modern concepts and new, alternative concepts produced in the clash. These constitute valuable material for rethinking political theory and imagining different democratic ways of living together. To do this, it is necessary to investigate concrete social and political events with the patience of the historian and, at the same time, to consider these events as unfinished experiments, with political passion and the attention of the philosopher to the possible.

Theory must keep open the incompleteness of these experiments, even when they appear to have been concluded or failed. With humility, theory must extract new concepts produced in the practice of nameless insurgents and consider these insurgents as colleagues whose practice is theory in action. They are the ones truly excluded from the canon of political thought.

ACKNOWLEDGMENTS

This book has benefited from numerous discussions. The chapter on the sanctuary was initially presented at the international workshop Sanctuary and Subjectivity held at the University of California, Santa Cruz, in 2018. It was subsequently revised and discussed at the conference on Anachronism at the University of Padova in 2019. Two chapters were written and discussed during my stay at the Shelby Cullom Davis Center at the Department of History, Princeton University, in 2020–2021. I wish to thank the director, David Bell, and all my colleagues who engaged with me on parts of this work. The chapter on property was discussed in May 2023 in Berlin with colleagues from the Colloquium Sozialphilosophie coordinated by Rahel Jaeggi at the Centre for Social Critique. My heartfelt thanks to Rahel for the insightful discussions both in Berlin and Santa Cruz. The introduction was discussed in 2023 with colleagues from the Committee on Globalization and Social Change at the Graduate Center (CUNY). My debt to the friends of the committee extends far beyond this work. A special thanks to Marcela Olivera, who generously shared all the materials I needed and was an invaluable interlocutor while I was writing the second chapter.

Among the many who contributed with their critical observations and comments, I especially acknowledge the conversations with Joan Scott and the ongoing dialogue with Anne Norton and Uday Mehta. The list could go on. Therefore, I wish to acknowledge, in no particular order but as they come to mind: Dale Tomich, whose sudden passing meant the loss of a wonderful interlocutor, an exceptional scholar, and a dear friend; Silvestre Gristina; Susan Buck-Morss; Gary Wilder; Mauro Farnesi Cammellone; Andrea Messner; Zahid Chaudhary; Andrea Cengia; Chiara Collamatti; Agnese Bellina; Robert Nichols; Harry Harootunian; Tamis Peixoto Parron; Duncan Faherty; Herman Bennett; Claire Bishop; Benjamin Davis; George Shulman; my students at UCSC, for their thoughtful questions and valuable insights; and many others who directly or indirectly contributed to the maturation of this book's theses. I want to thank Shaun Terry, who helped me with the index and with whom I also had the pleasure of discussing parts of this project.

I extend my gratitude to Thomas Lay and Jacques Lezra for their enthusiastic support in publishing *Revolution and Restoration* in the Idiom series of Fordham University Press. Rafaella Capanna helped me make this book more accessible to the English-speaking public.

Finally, I extend my deepest gratitude to my partner Banu Bargu, not only for encouraging me to complete the work when I was on the verge of setting it aside for a new project but especially for always being the most important and cherished part of my life. My two sons, Carlo and Teoman Paolo, with their life and actions, help me believe there is hope in this world.

NOTES

INTRODUCTION. THE WORK OF ANACHRONISM AND THE CONFIGURATION OF NEW CONCEPTS

The epigraph in the original German reads: "Das gute Neue ist niemals ganz neu. Es kommt nicht aus der hohlen Hand oder aus einem scheinbar freischwebenden Kopf." Ernst Bloch, *Tübinger Einleitung in die Philosophie* (Suhrkamp Verlag, 1970), 147.

1. Ernst Bloch, *Natural Law and Human Dignity* (MIT Press, 1987).

2. Vincent W. Lloyd, *Black Natural Law* (Oxford University Press, 2016), xi. On the modern colonial representations of the "human," see Sylvia Wynter, "Unsettling the Coloniality of Being/Power/Truth/Freedom: Towards the Human, After Man, Its Overrepresentation—an Argument," *CR: The New Centennial Review* 3, no. 3 (2003): 257–337.

3. Joan Scott, *Only Paradoxes to Offer: French Feminists and the Rights of Man* (Harvard University Press, 1996).

4. Thomas Spence, *The Restorer of Society to Its Natural State* (1801), in *Pigs' Meat: Selected Writings of Thomas Spence* (Spokesman, 1982), 127–65.

5. Joan Scott, *Sex and Secularism* (Princeton University Press, 2018), has shown how the concept of secularism has always worked as polemical concept, one closely interwoven with the regulation of sexuality and gender.

6. Reflections along these lines of research are becoming increasingly common. See Catherine Colliot-Thélène, *La démocratie sans 'demos'* (PUF, 2010); Mauro Farnesi Camellone, *Indocili soggetti. La politica teologica di Thomas Hobbes* (Quodlibet, 2013); Jacques Rancière, *On the Shores of Politics* (Verso, 2021); Anne Norton, *Wild Democracy: Anarchy, Courage, and Ruling the Law* (Oxford University Press, 2023).

7. Robespierre, June 14, 1793, *Archives parlementaires*, vol. 66, 530. *Archives parlementaires de 1789 à 1860: recueil complet des débats législatifs & politiques des Chambres françaises* (Paris: Librairie administrative de P. Dupont, 1862–), https://searchworks.stanford.edu/view/1071767.

8. Lucien Jaume, *Le discours jacobin et la démocratie* (Fayard, 1989), 299–307.

9. See Paul Friedland, *Political Actors: Representative Bodies and Theatricality in the Age of the French Revolution* (Cornell University Press, 2002), 290.

10. Jean Varlet, "Proposal for a Special and Imperative Mandate" (1792), in *Social and Political Thought of the French Revolution* (Peter Lang, 2001), 154.

11. Le Chapelier Law (June 14, 1791), in John Hall Stewart, *A Documentary Survey of the French Revolution* (Macmillan, 1951), 165–66, https://revolution.chnm.org/items/show/480.

12. *Archives parlementaires*, first series, vol. 39, March 6, 1792, 423–24.

13. *Le Moniteur Universel*, 31 Ottobre 1793, 163, https://diginole.lib.fsu.edu/islandora/object/fsu%3A387000#page/4/mode/2up.

14. Karl Marx, *The Jewish Question*, in *Early Writings* (Penguin, 1992), 232.

15. Marx, *The Jewish Question*, 233.

16. "You don't need to go to America to see savages" wrote Balzac in his *Paysans* (1844). See Eugen Weber, *Peasants Into Frenchmen* (Stanford University Press, 1976), 3.

17. There is nothing more terrible than a class of barbaric slaves which has learned to regard its existence as an injustice and which sets out to take revenge, not just for itself but for all future generations." Friedrich Nietzsche, The Birth of Tragedy and Other Writings (Cambridge University Press, 1990), 87.

18. Neil Hertz, "Medusa's Head: Male Hysteria Under Political Pressure," *Representations* 4 (1983): 27–54.

19. *OED*, https://www.oed.com/view/Entry/196393?redirectedFrom=synchronism#eid

20. Reinhart Koselleck, *Futures Past: On the Semantics of Historical Time* (Columbia University Press, 2004), 9–10.

21. Koselleck, *Futures Past*, 10.

22. Koselleck, *Futures Past*, 11.

23. In the Middle Ages there is not a unique time "but rather a whole spectrum of social rhythms modulated by regularities inherent in a various component process and by the nature of various human collectives." These temporal rhythms constitute "a hierarchy of social times within the given system." A. J. Gurevich, *Categories of Medieval Culture* (Routledge & Kegan Paul, 1985), 144.

24. Erich Auerbach, *Mimesis* (Princeton University Press, 2013), 555.

25. Carlo Mamani Condori, *Los Aymara frente a la historia: Dos ensayos metodológicos* (Ayuwiyri, 1992), 15. In the Quechua term *Pachakuti*, *pacha* can be translated as "space-time," and *kuti* means "return" or also "to turn over." See Karl Swinehart, "Decolonial Time in Bolivia's Pachakuti," *Signs and Society* 7, no. 1 (Winter 2019): pp. 96–114.

26. Condori, *Los Aymara*, 11.

27. Silvia Rivera Cusicanqui, *Violencias (re)encubiertas en Bolivia* (Editorial Piedra Rota, 2010), 51. The term *nayrapacha* can be translated as "ancient times," but not relating to a dead and concluded past but rather a past that implies the reversibility of the world-present and can therefore also be future. See Condori, *Los Aymaras*, 14; Pablo Uc, *Tinku y Pachakuti. Geopolíticas indígenas originarias y estado plurinacional en Bolivia* (Clacso, 2019), 31–56.

28. Karl Marx, *Grundrisse*, in *Marx/Engels Collected Works* (International Publishers, 1986), 28:43.

29. Jacques Rancière, "The Concept of Anachronism and the Historian's Truth" *InPrint* 3, no. 1 (2015), art. 3.

30. Jacques Le Goff, *Time, Work, and Culture in the Middle Ages* (University of Chicago Press, 1980), 46.

31. Le Goff, *Time, Work, and Culture*, 49–50.

32. E. P. Thompson, *Customs in Common* (New Press, 1993), 33.

33. Massimiliano Tomba, *Marx's Temporalities* (Brill, 2013), 136.

34. In the nineteenth century, with the expansion of the railway network, the need arose to synchronize various local clocks; the radio played a fundamental role in this synchronization. The definition of a World Standard Time in 1884 was the result of an agreement between states. Just look at the states or entire continents, such as Africa, that were excluded from the International Meridian Conference, which took place in Washington, DC, to get an idea of the power dynamics underlying this temporalization.

35. Thompson, *Customs in Common*.

36. G. W. F. Hegel, *Phenomenology of Spirit* (Oxford University Press, 1977), 289.

37. Daniel Bensaïd, *The Dispossessed: Karl Marx's Debates on Wood Theft and the Right of the Poor* (University of Minnesota Press, 2021); see Robert Nichols, "Crisis and Kleptocracy," in Bensaïd, *The Dispossessed*, vii–xxxiv.

38. As Arendt noticed, "The end of a tradition does not necessarily mean that traditional concepts have lost their power over the minds of men." Hannah Arendt, *Between Past and Future* (Viking, 1961), 26.

39. Kevin Whelan, *The Tree of Liberty: Radicalism, Catholicism, and the Construction of Irish Identity, 1760–1830* (Cork University Press, 1996), 56.

40. "The history of 'The Middle Ages' begins at the precise moment when European imperial and colonial expansion begins." There is a relationship between the Middle Ages as Europe's Dark Continent of History and Africa as Dark Ages of Geography: John Dagenais and Margaret R. Greer, "Decolonizing the Middle Ages: Introduction," *Journal of Medieval and Early Modern Studies* 30 (2000): 431–48. The authors claim that if colonization can take place in time as well in space, "the Middle Ages is a colonized region within the history of Modernity" (438).

41. As Kathleen Davis pointed out, the "idea of a 'feudal' past for Europe emerged

in legal battles over sovereignty." "The *becoming-feudal* of the Middle Ages . . . is the narrative and conceptual basis of 'modern' politics." Kathleen Davis, *Periodization and Sovereignty: How Ideas of Feudalism and Secularization Govern the Politics of Time* (University of Pennsylvania Press, 2008), 6, 25.

42. The notion of "internal colonialism," as recently reelaborated by Luis Tapia, can and should be extended to Europe's own internal history. Luis Tapia, *Dialéctica del colonialism interno* (Traficantes de Sueños, 2022). On the origin of the concept, see Pablo Gonzalez Casanova, "Internal Colonialism and National Development," *Studies in Comparative International Development* 1, no. 4 (1965): 27–37.

43. Gilles Deleuze and Félix Guattari, *What Is Philosophy?* (Columbia University Press, 1996), 61.

44. Massimiliano Tomba, "1525. The Insurgent Theology of the German Peasants," in *The History of the Present*, forthcoming.

45. Koselleck errs in defining the polemical nature of concepts as if it were almost one of their inherent characteristics. Consequently, he believes that their self-definition would also produce counterconcepts, which he dates back to ancient Greece in the pair Hellenes/Barbarians. Koselleck, *Futures Past*, 155–91.

46. Friedrich Hölderlin, "Das Werden im Vergehen," in *Sämtliche Werke. Historisch-kritische Ausgabe*, ed. Friedrich Beißner (Kohlhammer, 1962), 4.1:282.

47. Walter Benjamin, *The Arcades Project* (Harvard University Press, 1999), N8,1.

48. Ernst Bloch, *The Principle of Hope* (MIT Press, 1996), 1:8–9.

49. Alasdair MacIntyre, *After Virtue* (University of Notre Dame Press, 1984), 222.

50. Hans Freyer, *Theorie des gegenwärtige Zeitalters* (Deutsche Verlags-Anstalt, 1955), 177.

51. Fryer, *Theorie des gegenwaertige Zeitalters*, 7; Reinhart Koselleck, *Zeitschichten (Suhrkamp, 2003)*, 9.

52. Ernst Bloch, "Nonsynchronism and the Obligation to Its Dialectics" (1932), *New German Critique* 11 (Spring 1977).

53. Tomba, *Insurgent Universality*, 195.

54. According to Habermas, the council democracy and voluntary association "already practiced in the petit bourgeois revolution of the sansculottes" were always utopian and today even "less workable, given the regulatory and organizational needs of modern societies." Jürgen Habermas, *Between Facts and Norms: Contributions to a Discourse Theory of Law and Democracy* (MIT Press, 1996), 480–1. Similarly, Martin Jay argues that the councils are dead and "what the left used to sneer at as 'bourgeois democracy' . . . has shown itself more resilient and responsive to the need of its constituency . . . than other alternatives." Martin Jay, "No Power to the Soviets," *Salmagundi* 88/89 (1990–1991): 67–68. For a critical analysis of the categories of progress and regression, see Rahel Jaeggi, *Fortschritt und Regression* (Suhrkamp, 2023).

1. REVOLUTION AND RESTORATION

1. Victor Hugo, *Les misérables* (Machette, 2003), 3:67.

2. Michael Löwy, ed., *Révolutions* (Hazan, 2000); *Revolutions* (Haymarket, 2020).

3. Löwy, *Revolutions*, 532.

4. *Zapatistas! Documents of the New Mexican Revolution* (Autonomedia, 1994), 340.

5. G. W. F. Hegel, *Hegel and the Human Spirit: A Translation of the Jena Lectures on the Philosophy of Spirit (1805–6)* (Wayne State University Press, 1983), 155.

6. Massimiliano Tomba, *Insurgent Universality: An Alternative Legacy of Modernity* (Oxford University Press, 2019).

7. Comandanta Esther y María de Jesús Patricio, "La ley actual, no la de la COCOPA discrimina a las mujeres," *Triple Jornada*, April 2, 2001.

8. Souad Eddouada, "Land Rights and Women's Rights in Morocco: Cooperation and Contestation Among Rural and Urban Women Activists," *History of the Present* 11 (2021): 23–52.

9. Reinhart Koselleck, "Hinweise auf die temporalen Strukturen begriffsgeschichtlichen Wandels," in *Begriffsgeschichten: Studien zur Semantik und Pragmatik der politischen und sozialen Sprache* (Suhrkamp Verlag, 2006), 90.

10. *OED*, https://www.oed.com/view/Entry/163986; see also "Petitions in the State Papers: 1660s," British History Online, https://www.british-history.ac.uk/petitions/state-papers/1660s#highlight-first.

11. Thomas Hobbes, *Behemoth* (Oxford University Press, 2010), 389–90: "I have seen in this revolution a circular motion of the Sovereign Power through two Usurpers Father and Son, from the late King to this his Son. For (leaving out the power of the Council of Officers, which was but temporary, and no otherwise owned by them but in trust) it moved from King Charles the first to the Long Parliament, from thence to the Rump, from the Rump to Oliver Cromwell, and then back again from Richard Cromwell to the Rump, thence to the long Parliament, and thence to King Charles the second, where long may it remain."

12. Keith M. Baker, "Revolutionizing Revolution," in Keith M. Baker and Dan Edelstein, *Scripting Revolution* (Stanford University Press, 2015), 74–75.

13. Cited in Thomas Kuhn, *The Copernican Revolution* (Harvard University Press, 1992), 191.

14. Karl Griewank, *Der neuzeitliche Revolutionsbegriff* (Europäische Verlagsanstalt, 1969), 104–5.

15. Maiolino Bisaccioni, *Historia delle guerre civili de gli ultimi tempi* (Venezia: Francesco Storti, 1652), 1.

16. Dante, *Convivio*, II, XIV, https://digitaldante.columbia.edu/text/library/the-convivio/book-02/#14.

17. On the inadequacy of the modern differentiation between "line" and "circle" concerning the way the ancients perceived historical time, see Santo Mazzarino, *Il pensiero storico classico* (Laterza, 1990), 3:416–7.

18. Arnaldo Momigliano, *La storiografia greca* (Einaudi, 1982), 76–81. Momigliano writes that outside the constitutional chapters, "Polybius operates as if he had no cyclical conception of history. . . . Individual events are judged either on the basis of vague notions, such as luck, or on the basis of more precise criteria of wisdom and human competence" (80).

19. Reinhart Koselleck, *Futures Past: On the Semantics of Historical Time* (Columbia University Press, 2004), 28.

20. Nicoló Machiavelli, *Discourses* (University of Chicago Press, 1998), I, 2, p. 11.

21. Girolamo Savonarola, *Selected Writings: Religion and Politics, 1490–1498* (Yale University Press, 2006), 183.

22. Savonarola, *Selected Writings*, 196.

23. Koselleck, *Futures Past*, 46.

24. Koselleck, *Futures Past*, 47.

25. Reinhart Koselleck, "Revolution, Rebellion, Aufruhr, Bürgerkrieg," in *Geschichtliche Grundbegriffe, 1984*, 5:734–37; Koselleck, *Futures Past*, p. 51.

26. Condorcet, *The Sketch*, in *Political Writings* (Cambridge University Press, 2012), 146.

27. Condorcet, *The Sketch*, 146.

28. Immanuel Kant, *The Contest of the Faculties*, in *Toward the Perpetual Peace and Other Writings on Politics, Peace and History* (Yale University Press, 2006), 150.

29. Koselleck, *Futures Past*, 267.

30. Kant, *The Contest of the Faculties*, 155.

31. Kant, *The Contest of the Faculties*, 155.

32. Kant, *The Contest of the Faculties*, 162.

33. Kant, *The Contest of the Faculties*, 162.

34. Kant, *The Contest of the Faculties*, 189.

35. Le Chapelier Law (June 14, 1791), in John Hall Stewart, *A Documentary Survey of the French Revolution* (Macmillan, 1951), 165–66, https://revolution.chnm.org/items/show/480.

36. William H. Sewell, *Work and Revolution in France: The Language of Labor from the Old Regime to 1848* (Cambridge University Press, 1980), 182: "In many respects, then, workers' corporations of the nineteenth century carried on the themes, the organizational forms, the values, and the practices of corporations of the old regime. But these familiar elements of old-regime corporations now stood in a different relation to each other and to the outside world."

37. Jorge Sánches Morales, *La revolución rural francesa. Libertad, igualdad y comunidad (1789–1793)* (Biblioteca Nueva, 2017).

38. Albert Soboul, *The French Revolution, 1789–1799* (Vintage, 1975), 332. Soboul defined the popular movement of the sans-culottes as "characterized by the pre-capitalist mentality . . . a mentality that was essentially the same as that of the peasantry who were bitterly defending their common-land rights against the onslaught of capitalist agricultural methods."

39. Rafe Blaufarb, *The Great Demarcation: The French Revolution and the Invention of Modern Property* (Oxford University Press, 2016), 128.

40. Oswald Spengler, *Letters, 1913–1936* (George Allen & Unwin, 1966), 68–71.

41. Oswald Spengler, "Pessimism?," in *Prussian Socialism and Other Essays* (Black House, 2018), 142.

42. Bruno Bauer, *Geschichte Deutschlands und der französischen Revolution unter der Herrschaft Napoleons* (E. Bauer Verlag, 1846), 2:68.

43. Michael Pauen, *Pessimismus: Geschichtsphilosophie, Metaphysik und Moderne von Nietzsche bis Spengler* (Akademie Verlag, 1997).

44. Furio Jesi, *Spartakus: The Symbology of Revolt* (Seagull, 2014), 46.

45. Gustav Landauer, "The United Republics of Germany and Their Constitution," in *All Power to the Councils: A Documentary History of the German Revolution of 1918–1919*, ed. G. Kuhn (PM, 2012), 200.

46. Edgar Julius Jung, "Deutschland und die konservative Revolution," in *Deutsche über Deutschland: Die Stimme des unbekannten Politikers* (A. Langen, 1932), 380.

47. Federico Marcon, "Fascism's Counterrevolutionary Revolution," unpublished paper presented at the Shelby Cullom Davis Center for Historical Studies, Princeton University, October 2, 2020.

48. Landauer, "The United Republics of Germany and Their Constitution," 200–1.

49. Landauer, "The United Republics of Germany and Their Constitution," 201.

50. Carl Schmitt, *Constitutional Theory (Duke University Press, 2008)*, 251.

51. J. S. Mill, *On Liberty and Other Writings* (Cambridge University Press, 1989), 13; J. S. Mill, *Considerations on Representative Government*, in *The Collected Works* (Toronto University Press, 1977), 19:335–36; Uday S. Mehta, *Liberalism and Empire: A Study in Nineteenth-Century British Liberal Thought* (University of Chicago Press, 1999).

52. Peter Burke, "The Renaissance Sense of Anachronism," in *Die Renaissance als erste Aufklärung*, ed. Enno Rolph (Mohr Siebeck Verlag, 1998), 3:21.

53. George H. Sabine, *The Works of Gerrard Winstanley* (Cornell University Press, 1941), 252.

54. Sabine, *The Works of Gerrard Winstanley*, 260.

55. "The New Law of Righteousness," in Sabine, *The Works of Gerrard Winstanley*, 159.

56. Sabine, *The Works of Gerrard Winstanley*, 305–6.

57. Sabine, *The Works of Gerrard Winstanley*, 408, 292.

58. Sabine, *The Works of Gerrard Winstanley*, 303.

59. Sabine, *The Works of Gerrard Winstanley*, 159.

60. Thomas Spence, *The Restorer of Society to Its Natural State* (1801), in *Pigs' Meat: Selected Writings of Thomas Spence* (Spokesman, 1982), 127–65.

61. Spence, *The Restorer of Society*, 151.

62. Sabine, *The Works of Gerrard Winstanley*, 533, 589, 559.

63. "El desembarco," Enlace Zapatista, http://enlacezapatista.ezln.org.mx/2021/06/23/el-desembarco/.

2. PRIVATE AND SOCIAL PROPERTY

1. Robert Albro, "The Culture of Democracy and Bolivia's Indigenous Movements," *Critique of Anthropology* 26, no. 4 (2006): 390–92.

2. Alexander Dwinell and Marcela Olivera, "The Water Is Ours Damn It! Water Commoning in Bolivia," *Community Development Journal* 49 (2014): 147.

3. The arrival of the Spanish is dated 1532. Sinclair Thomson, *We Alone Will Rule: Native Andean Politics in the Age of Insurgency* (University of Wisconsin Press, 2002), 27–63.

4. José Flores Moncayo, *Legislación boliviana del indio. Recopilación de resoluciones, órdenes, decretos, leyes, decretos supremos y otras disposiciones legales, 1825–1953* (Departamento de Publicaciones del Instituto Indigenista Boliviano, 1953), 226; Laura Gotkowitz, *A Revolution for Our Rights: Indigenous Struggles for Land and Justice in Bolivia, 1880–1952* (Duke University Press, 2007), 6.

5. Gotkowitz, *A Revolution for Our Rights*, 30–31: "The 1874 law paved the way for the most devastating assault against communal property since the seventeenth century. . . . In 1880, Indian communities held approximately half of Bolivia's farmland; by 1930, the communities' holdings had been diminished to less than a third."

6. Sinclair, *We Alone Will Rule*, 76. See also Irene Silverblatt, *Moon, Sun, and Witches: Gender Ideologies and Class in Inca and Colonial Peru* (Princeton University Press, 1987), 111: The "Spanish conquest introduced to the Andes new concepts of property ownership and land tenure, along with a complex legal system through which these forms were maintained and transmitted."

7. Silverblatt, *Moon, Sun, and Witches*, 111, 119. Silverblatt continues: "According to Spanish law, wives could not freely dispose of their property, and Andean custom contradicted the law in this area. Andean tradition, still followed today, maintained that women, regardless of marital status, held independent rights over all goods, including lands, that might be inherited or otherwise acquired. The concept of joint or common property did not exist" (119–20). See Sinclair, *We Alone Will Rule*, 34–35, 70–82.

8. Two Lawyers from La Paz, "Transforming the Property Regime," in *The Boli-*

via Reader: History, Culture, Politics, ed. S. Thomas et al. (Duke University Press, 2018), 181.

9. Thomas et al., *The Bolivia Reader*, 182.

10. The 1953 agrarian reform law stated that every individual, without distinction of sex, is entitled to benefit from agrarian and land settlement programs; "customary norms and practices, however, show a strong bias against women owning land." Susana Lastarria-Cornhiel, "Land Tenure, Titling, and Gender in Bolivia," *Saint Louis University Public Law Review* 29, no. 1 (2009): 220.

11. Silvia Rivera Cusicanqui, "Liberal Democracy and Ayllu Democracy in Bolivia: The Case of Northern Potosí," *Journal of Development Studies* 26 (1990): 97–121.

12. Willem Assies, "Land Tenure Legislation in a Pluri-cultural and Multi-ethnic Society: The Case of Bolivia," *Journal of Peasant Studies* 33, no. 4 (2006): 599.

13. The first article of the law states: "The present Law acknowledges, promotes, and consolidates the process of Popular Participation, incorporating the indigenous communities, indigenous peoples, rural communities and urban neighbourhoods in the juridical, political and economic life of the country. . . . It strengthens the political and economic means and institutions necessary for perfecting representative democracy, incorporating citizens' participation in a process of participative democracy and guaranteeing equality of representation at all levels between women and men." Government of Bolivia, 1994; author's translation. See David Altman and Rickard Lalander, "Bolivia's Popular Participation Law: An Undemocratic Democratisation Process?," in *Decentralisation and Democratic Governance: Experiences from India, Bolivia and South Africa*, ed. Axel Hadenius (Almqvist & Wiksell International, 2003), 70.

14. In 1994, a neighborhood leader expressed the following criticism: "But what happens with the Popular Participation Law? Each neighbourhood committee is empowered to make its own arrangements with the state without consulting any overarching organization. The intentions of the government are to divide and rule. It intends to debilitate the main organizations by putting local leaders in charge of small areas and [tying them directly to the state]. This guarantees that there are no solid institutions that question the government. It reduces the power of the popular movement." In Altman and Lalander, "Bolivia's Popular Participation Law," 81.

15. Jose Antonio Lucero, *Struggles of Voice: The Politics of Indigenous Representation in the Andes* (University of Pittsburgh Press, 2008), 167.

16. "Bolivia: Ley de Agua Potable y Alcantarillado Sanitario, 29 de octubre de 1999," Lexivox, https://www.lexivox.org/norms/BO-L-2029.html.

17. "Bolivia: Ley de Agua Potable y Alcantarillado Sanitario, 29 de octubre de 1999."

18. Cited in Alvaro García, Raquel Gutiérrez, Raúl Prada, and Luis Tapia, *El retorno de la Bolivia plebeya* (Muela del Diablo Editores, 2000), 142.

19. Oscar Olivera, *¡Cochabamba! Water War in Bolivia* (South End, 2004), 9.

20. Carwil Bjork-James, *The Sovereign Street: Making Revolution in Urban Bolivia* (University of Arizona Press, 2020), 67–85.

21. William Finnegan, "Leasing the Rain," *New Yorker*, March 31, 2002, https://www.newyorker.com/magazine/2002/04/08/leasing-the-rain.

22. Olivera, *¡Cochabamba!*, 156.

23. Raquel Gutiérrez-Aguilar, "The Coordinadora. One Year After the Water War," in Olivera, *¡Cochabamba!*, 60.

24. *¡Y . . . el agua sigue siendo nuestra!*, Cochabamba, February 6, 2000.

25. *¡¡Basta de sufrimiento social!!*, Cochabamba, 2000.

26. *"¡El agua es nuestra, carajo!,"* Cochabamba, January 27, 2000.

27. See, for example, the case of women in Turkey and Kurdistan: Nazan Üstündağ, "Mother, Politician, and Guerilla: The Emergence of a New Political Imagination in Kurdistan Through Women's Bodies and Speech," *Differences: A Journal of Feminist Cultural Studies* 30, no. 2 (2019): 115–45.

28. Vivienne Bennett, Sonia Dávila-Poblete, and María Nieves Rico, "Water and Gender: The Unexpected Connection That Really Matters," *Journal of International Affairs* 61, no. 2 (2008): 121–22: "After the Cochabamba Water War, when people returned to normal life, many women who had participated in the protests described profound changes in their identity as community members, especially relative to their participation in activities that would have been off-limits to them prior to the water war. . . . Participation cannot be mandated by decree; it is part of a profound cultural change that has to permeate all social actors." See also Rocío Bustamante, Elizabeth Peredo, and María Esther Udaeta, "Women in the 'Water War' in the Cochabamba Valleys," in *The Politics of Water and Gender in Latin America*, ed. Vivienne Bennett et al. (University of Pittsburgh Press, 2005), 79.

29. Alvaro García, Raquel Gutiérrez, Raúl Prada, and Luis Tapia, "La forma multitud de la política de las necesidades vitales," in *El retorno de la Bolivia plebeya*, 170.

30. García, Gutiérrez, Prada, and Tapia, "La forma multitud de la política de las necesidades vitales," 170.

31. *¡Y . . . el agua sigue siendo nuestra!*, Cochabamba, February 6, 2000.

32. García, Gutiérrez, Prada, and Tapia, "La forma multitud de la política de las necesidades vitales," 181.

33. Sarah T. Hines, *Water for All: Community, Property, and Revolution in Modern Bolivia* (University of California Press, 2022), 15, calls *"vernacular modernism"* the Cochabambino water users' "creative appropriation and adaptation of modernist development paradigms from below on practitioners' own terms." She continues: "While high modernism requires ignoring local history, knowledge, people, and ecology, vernacular modernists draw on their knowledge of history and ecology to advocate for

fulfillment of modernity's promises. Unlike authoritarian high modernism, vernacular modernism aims to democratize modernism and indeed modernity itself" (15). On the "messy democracy," see Uday Mehta and Massimiliano Tomba, "Messy Democracy as Practice and Attitude," forthcoming. On vernacularized politics and democracy, see Sian Lazar, *El Alto, Rebel City: Self and Citizenship in Andean Bolivia* (Duke University Press, 2008), 234; on the emergence of vernacular democracies that challenge the normative conception of democracy, see David Nugent, "Democracy Otherwise: Struggles Over Popular Rule in the Northern Peruvian Andes," in *Democracy: Anthropological Approaches*, ed. Julia Paley (School for Advanced Research Press, 2008), 21–62. From a different perspective and a different geographic area, on the "vernacular ideas of popular sovereignty" that undermine liberal rights in the name of "the law of force" instead of "the force of law," see Thomas Blom Hansen, "Democracy Against the Law: Reflections on India's Illiberal Democracy," in *Majoritarian State: How Hindu Nationalism Is Changing India*, ed. A. P. Chatterji, T. B. Hansen, and C. Jaffrelot (Oxford University Press, 2019), 19–39.

34. Olivera, *¡Cochabamba!*, 57.

35. Albro, "The Culture of Democracy and Bolivia's Indigenous Movements," 390–92.

36. Raquel Gutiérrez-Aguilar, *Rhythms of the Pachakuti* (Duke University Press, 2014), xxii.

37. Lucia Linsalata, *Cuando manda la asamblea. Lo comunitario-popular en Bolivia: una aproximación desde los sistemas comunitarios de agua de Cochabamba*, Tesis para optar por el grado académico de Doctora en Estudios Latinoamericanos, México D.F., UNAM, 2014, 102. The dissertation was also published by SOCEE (Sociedad Comunitaria de Estudios Estratégicos) in 2015.

38. "[I] reappropriate what is ours; [II] reappropriate our rights; [III] reappropriate the patrimony of the country; [IV] reappropriate the ability to say and to do, decide and execute the projects and plans that suit the people and the country." "*¡El agua es nuestra, carajo! Vocero official de la Coordinadora de Defensa del Agua y la Vida*," January 2000, vol. 1, no. 1.

39. Forrest Hylton and Sinclair Thomson, *Revolutionary Horizons: Past and Present in Bolivian Politics (Verso, 2007)*, 26–30.

40. Sivia Rivera Cusicanqui, "Aymara Past, Aymara Future," *Report on the Americas* 25 (1991): 21.

41. Aguillar, *Rhythms of the Pachakuti*, 50.

42. García, Gutiérrez, Prada, and Tapia, "La forma multitud de la política de las necesidades vitales," 177.

43. Oscar Olivera, in Linsalata, *Cuando manda la asamblea*, 170; Aguillar, *Rhythms of the Pachakuti*, 51.

44. 2000 Declaration, https://www.nadir.org/nadir/initiativ/agp/free/imf/bolivia /cochabamba.htm#declaration. An English translation of the Cochabamba Declaration is also available in Olivera, *¡Cochabamba!*.

45. García, Gutiérrez, Prada, and Tapia, "La forma multitud de la política de las necesidades vitales," 172.

46. Linsalata, *Cuando manda la asamblea*, 124.

47. Linsalata, *Cuando manda la asamblea*, 124.

48. Thomas et al., *The Bolivia Reader*, 38.

49. Linsalata, *Cuando manda la asamblea*, 102.

50. Agnese Bellina, "A Novel Way of Being Together? On the Depoliticising Effects of Attributing Rights to Nature," *Environmental Politics* (2023), https://doi.org/10 .1080/09644016.2023.2209005.

51. Willem Assies, "David Versus Goliath in Cochabamba: Water Rights, Neoliberalism, and the Revival of Social Protest in Bolivia," *Latin American Perspectives* 30, no. 3 (2003): 30.

52. Susan Spronk, "Roots of Resistance to Urban Water Privatization in Bolivia: The 'New Working Class,' the Crisis of Neoliberalism, and Public Services," *International Labor and Working-Class History* 71 (2007): 8–28; Nasya S. Razavi, "'Social Control' and the Politics of Public Participation in Water Remunicipalization, Cochabamba, Bolivia," *Water* 11 (2019): 1–19.

53. Linsalata, *Cuando manda la asamblea*, 180.

54. Raquel Gutiérrez-Aguilar, "The Coordinadora: One Year After the Water War," in Olivera, *¡Cochabamba!*, 60.

55. On the appropriation of water and SEMAPA by the state, see Carlos Crespo Flores, "Estatalizacion del agua en Bolivia," *El Libertario* 76 (2015), http://periodicoellibertario.blogspot.com/2011/12/estatalizacion-del-agua-en-bolivia .html.

56. Universal Declaration of the Rights of Mother Earth, https://www.garn.org/wp -content/uploads/2024/02/ENG-Universal-Declaration-of-the-Rights-of-Mother-Earth.pdf

57. Universal Declaration of the Rights of Mother Earth.

58. Universal Declaration of the Rights of Mother Earth.

59. Law of the Rights of Mother Earth, http://archive.wphna.org/wp-content /uploads/2014/07/2010-12-07-Bolivian-Law-of-rights-of-Mother-Earth.pdf.

60. Bolivia's Constitution of 2009, https://www.constituteproject.org/constitution /Bolivia_2009.pdf.

61. Ana Carolina Delgado, "The TIPNIS Conflict in Bolivia," *Contexto Internacional* 39, no. 2 (May–August 2017): 373–91; Ricardo Calla, "TIPNIS y Amazonia: Contradicciones en la agenda ecológica de Bolivia," *European Review of Latin American and Caribbean Studies* 91 (2011): 77–83.

62. Dan Collyns, "Bolivia Approves Highway Through Amazon Biodiversity

Hotspot," *Guardian*, August 15, 2017, https://www.theguardian.com/environment /2017/aug/15/bolivia-approves-highway-in-amazon-biodiversity-hotspot-as-big-as -jamaica.

63. Article 30 provides indigenous people the right to "self-determination and territoriality" (Art. 30.II.4.), "the collective ownership of land and territories" (Art. 30.II.6), and "to be consulted by appropriate procedures, in particular through their institutions" (Art. 30.II.15).

64. Cited in Dewick Hindery, "Clashing Cosmologies and Constitutional Contradictions," in *From Enron to Evo: Pipeline Politics, Global Environmentalism, and Indigenous Rights in Bolivia* (University of Arizona Press, 2013), 178.

65. Nancy Postero, *The Indigenous State: Race, Politics, and Performance in Plurinational Bolivia* (University of California Press, 2017), 130.

66. Hindery, "Clashing Cosmologies and Constitutional Contradictions," 174.

67. "El punto de bifurcación es un momento en el que se miden ejércitos," interview with Álvaro García Linera by Maristella Svampa, Pablo Stefanoni, and Ricardo Bajo, *Le Monde Diplomatique* (Bolivia), February 9, 2009, https://rebelion.org/el -punto-de-bifurcacion-es-un-momento-en-el-que-se-miden-ejercitos/.

68. Álvaro García Linera, *Geopolítica de la Amazonía: Poder hacendal-patrimonial y acumulación capitalista*, La Paz, Bolivia, 2012, https://www .vicepresidencia.gob.bo/IMG/pdf/geopolitica_de_la_amazonia.pdf, 66.

69. In 2007, the Ecuadorian government declared that it would suspend the extraction of oil from a field within the Yasuni National Park, but in 2013 Rafael Correa's government announced that for economic reasons the extraction of oil had become necessary.

70. Jean-Jacques Rousseau, *The Social Contract* (Oxford University Press, 1994), 58.

71. Article 304, which should recognize rural native indigenous autonomies and authorities, clarifies the extent of this authority: "Irrigation systems, hydraulic resources, sources of water and energy, *within the framework of State policy*, within their territory" (Art. 304, III, 4).

72. John L. Hammond, "Indigenous Community Justice in the Bolivian Constitution of 2009," *Human Rights Quarterly* 33 (2011): 678. The principle stated by the court is that "customary law cannot violate the Constitution and the laws." This means that indigenous territories are not only not an autonomous jurisdiction from the state but are subject to forced institutionalization (*institucionalización forzada*) and state dominion of lands: Idon Moisés Chivi Vargas, "Justicia indígena y jurisdicción constitucional. Bolivia 2003–2004," *Derechos Humanos y Acción Defensorial* 1 (2006): 66–70.

73. C169—Indigenous and Tribal Peoples Convention, 2009, https://www.ilo.org /dyn/normlex/en/f?p=NORMLEXPUB:12100:0::NO::P12100_ILO_CODE:C169.

74. "An advanced Occidental law, wedded in its apotheosis to freedom and a certain equality, becomes thoroughly despotic when shipped to the rest of the world

in the formal colonizations from the late eighteenth to the early twentieth centuries."
Peter Fitzpatrick, *The Mythology of Modern Law* (Routledge, 1992), 107.

75. Garrett Hardin, "The Tragedy of the Commons," *Science* 162, no 3859 (1968): 1244.

76. It is a myth that yields on enclosed (private) land were significantly higher than on open (communal) fields. Historical facts collected at that time "do not support the conclusion that enclosures or capitalist farming caused the growth in English grain yields. That was just landlord ideology in the eighteenth century." Robert C. Allen and Cormac Ó Gráda, "On the Road Again with Arthur Young: English, Irish, and French Agriculture During the Industrial Revolution," *Journal of Economic History* 48, no. 1 (1988): 93–116. See also David A. Atwood, "Land Registration in Africa: The Impact on Agricultural Production," *World Development* 18, no. 5 (1990): 659–71. Atwood calls into question the conventional view that "traditional" systems of African land rights impeded agricultural development, whereas land titling would have encouraged land transfers to more productive farmers; Sjaastad and Bromley question the prejudice that a "nation with little wealth must be in want of land privatization." Instead, they find a "number of countries where traditional property regimes have not been shown to be failures." See also Espen Sjaastad and Daniel W. Bromley, "The Prejudices of Property Rights: On Individualism, Specificity, and Security in Property Regimes," *Development Policy Review* 18, no. 4 (2000): 365–89; Michael Kopsidis, Katja Bruisch, and Daniel W. Bromley, "Where Is the Backward Russian Peasant? Evidence Against the Superiority of Private Farming, 1883–1913," *Journal of Peasant Studies* 42, no. 2 (2015): 425–47.

77. The literature on the *commons* is enormous. I will mention only a few interpretive pieces: Elinor Ostrom, *Governing the Commons: The Evolution of Institutions for Collective Action* (Cambridge University Press, 1990); Peter Linebaugh, *Stop, Thief! The Commons, Enclosures, and Resistance* (PM, 2014); Ash Amin and Philip Howell, *Releasing the Commons: Rethinking the Futures of the Commons* (Routledge, 2016); Massimo De Angelis, *Omnia Sunt Communia: On the Commons and the Transformation to Postcapitalism* (Zed, 2017); Silvia Federici, *Re-enchanting the World: Feminism and the Politics of the Commons* (PM, 2018); David Bollier and Silke Helfrich, *Fair and Alive: The Insurgent Power of the Commons* (New Society, 2019); Pierre Dardot and Christian Laval, *Common: On Revolution in the 21st Century* (Bloomsbury, 2019); Vandana Shiva, *Reclaiming the Commons: Biodiversity, Indigenous Knowledge, and the Rights of Mother Earth* (Synergetic, 2020); Ian Angus, *The War Against the Commons: Dispossession and Resistance in the Making of Capitalism* (Monthly Review Press, 2023).

78. Carlo Cattaneo, *Sulla bonificazione del piano di Megadino* (1853), in *Scritti economici* (Le Monnier, 1956), 187, emphasis mine. Cattaneo was speaking of forms of management of collective forest and pasture resources that still exist in the Alps.

79. Emilio Morpurgo, Inchiesta Jacini. Atti della Giunta per la inchiesta agraria e sulle condizioni della classe agricola. Relazione del Commissario Comm. Emilio Morpurgo sulla XI Circoscrizione (provincie di Verona, Vicenza, Padova, Rovigo, Venezia, Treviso, Belluno e Udine) (Arnaldo Forni, 1979), 41, 45.

80. Paolo Grossi, *Il mondo delle terre collettive* (Quodlibet, 2019), 18, 39, 61–62.

81. Mark D. Steinberg, *Voices of Revolution, 1917* (Yale University Press, 2001), 143.

82. Steinberg, *Voices of Revolution, 1917*, 242.

83. Daniel de Coppet, ". . . Land Owns People," in *Context and Levels: Anthropological Essays on Hierarchy*, ed. R. H. Barnes, D. de Coppet, and M. J. Parkin (JASO, 1985), 30.

84. de Coppet, ". . . Land Owns People," 31.

85. Hugo Blanco, *We the Indians: The Indigenous Peoples of Peru and the Struggle for Land* (Merlin, 2018), 172.

86. Blanco, *We the Indians*, 172.

87. Linda Farthing and Ben Kohl, "Bolivia's New Wave of Protest," *NACLA Report on the Americas* 34, no. 5 (2001): 8–11.

88. Glen Sean Coulthard, *Red Skin, White Masks: Rejecting the Colonial Politics of Recognition* (University of Minnesota Press, 2014), 61. See also Allice Legat, *Walking the Land, Feeding the Fire: Knowledge and Stewardship Among the Tlicho Dene* (University of Arizona Press, 2012); Vine Deloria Jr, *God Is Red: A Native View of Religion* (Fulcrum, 2003), 271–86.

89. Felice Vaggioli, *History of New Zealand and Its Inhabitants* (University of Otago Press, 2000), 128.

90. Paolo Grossi, *L'inaugurazione della proprietà moderna* (Guida, 1980), 21–22; Paolo Grossi, *A History of European Law* (Wiley Blackwell, 2010), 2.

91. Paolo Grossi, *La proprietà e le proprietà nell'officina dello storico* (Editoriale Scientifica, 2006), 70–74.

92. Gilles Couvreur, *Les pauvres ont-ils des droits? Recherches sur le vol en cas d'extrême nécessité* (Presses de l'Université Grégorienne, 1961), 138.

93. Aron J. Gurevich, *Categories of Medieval Culture* (Routledge & Kegan Paul, 1985), 254: "Strictly speaking, the concept of 'private owner' cannot properly be applied either to the medieval landlord or to his vassal." The landowner, continues Gurevich, was not "possessor" but "holder" (*tenens*), and "the rights of the tenants were always limited." Feudal ownership must be understood as interpersonal form, not as a reified form of social relations.

94. G. W. F. Hegel, *Elements of the Philosophy of Right*, ed. Allen W. Wood, trans. H. B. Nisbet (Cambridge University Press, 1991), §§34–35. In relation to property, Hegel also used the term "absolute free will": G. W. F. Hegel, *The Philosophical Propaedeutic* (Basil Blackwell, 1986), 26.

95. Hegel, *Philosophy of Right*, §44.

96. Hegel, *Philosophy of Right*, §44.

97. Hegel, *Philosophy of Right*, §37 Z.

98. Thomas Paine, Letter Addressed to the Addressers on the Late Proclamation (London: Printed for H. D. Symonds, and Thomas Clio Rickman, 1792), 67, https://quod.lib.umich.edu/e/ecco/004809403.0001.000/1:2.

99. *The Summa Parisiensis on the Decretum Gratiani*, ed. by Terence P. McLaughlin, Toronto: PIMS, 1952, Distinctio VIII: ". . . jure divino omnia esse communia. . . . In rebus enim mundi nos usufructuarii et solus Deus proprietarius, scilicet quod naturalia sunt communia ut terra, aqua et hujusmodi in quibus aliquis habet usumfructum jure naturali, sed non proprietatem."

100. Thomas Aquinas, *Summa Theologiae*, II, II, 66.7, http://www.logicmuseum.com/wiki/Authors/Thomas_Aquinas/Summa_Theologiae/Part_IIb/Q66.

101. Aquinas, *Summa Theologiae*, II, II, 66. See Marco Bartoli, "Theft in Case of Need: Reflections on the Ethical-Economic Lexicon of the Middle Ages," *Journal for Markets and Ethics* 6, no. 1 (2018): 27–38.

102. Couvreur, *Les pauvres ont-ils des droits?*. I want to thank Warren Montag, who recalled my attention to Couvreur's text "The Prisoners of Starvation, or *Necessitas dat legem*," *New Formations* 89/90 (2016): 12–29.

103. Huguccio Pisanus, *Summa Decretum*, ed. by Oldrich Prerovský et al. (Biblioteca Apostolica Vaticana, 2006), ad C. 12, qu. 2, c. 11, v. ex inopia. Cited in Bartoli, "Theft in Case of Need," 36.

104. Huguccio, *Summa Decretum*, ad C. 12, qu. 2, c. 11, v. ex inopia.

105. Hegel, *Elements of the Philosophy of Right*, §127.

106. The court affirmed that "the condition of the accused and the circumstances in which the possession of the goods took place show that he took possession of that little food to meet an immediate and unavoidable need to feed himself, acting in a state of need." "Rubare per fame non integra il delitto di furto," *Giurisprudenza Penale*, May 16, 2016, https://www.giurisprudenzapenale.com/2016/05/16/rubare-fame-non-integra-delitto-furto/. This ruling attracted the attention of the US press: Gaia Pianigiani and Sewell Chan, "Can the Homeless and Hungry Steal Food? Maybe, an Italian Court Says," *New York Times*, May 3, 2016.

107. Hugo Grotius, *De iure belli ac pacis* (1625), book II, chap. 2, sec. 6, 4; *The Right of War and Peace* (Liberty Fund, 2005), 434–35: "Even amongst theologians it is a received opinion, that whoever shall take from another what is absolutely necessary for the preservation of his own life, is not from thence to be accounted guilty of theft (*furtum non committere*): of which rule the reason is, not that which some allege, that the owner of the thing is obliged to give so much to him that needs it, out of charity (*caritatis regula rem egenti dare tenetur*); but on this, that all things must be understood to be assigned to owners with some such benevolent exception, that in

such cases one might enter again upon the rights of the primitive community." Among the theologians to whom Grotius refers there is also Thomas, II.II.66.7.

108. Couvreur, *Les pauvres ont-ils des droits?*, 82.

109. Anton Lauterbach, *Tagebuch aus das Jahr 1538* (Dresden: Verlag von Justus Naumann's Buchhandlung, 1872), November 10, p. 165.

110. Thomas Spence, *Pigs' Meat: Selected Writings of Thomas Spence* (Spokesman, 1982), 60: "What we cannot live without we have the same property in as our lives."

111. John Locke, *Two Treatises of Government* (Yale University Press, 2003), §18, p. 107–8. Locke continues: "Thus a thief, whom I cannot harm, but by appeal to the law, for having stolen all that I am worth, I may kill, when he sets on me to rob me but of my horse or coat; because the law, which was made for my preservation, where it cannot interpose to secure my life from present force, which, if lost, is capable of no reparation, permits me my own defence, and the right of war, a liberty to kill the aggressor, because the aggressor allows not time to appeal to our common judge, nor the decision of the law, for remedy in a case where the mischief may be irreparable" (§19, p. 108).

112. Gerrard Winstanley, *Fire in the Bush*, in George H. Sabine, *The Works of Gerrard Winstanley* (Cornell University Press, 1941), 492.

113. Locke, *Two Treatises of Government*, §26, p. 111. See also Locke, §25, p. 111: "It is very clear, that God, as king David says, Psal. Cv x. 16, 'has given the earth to the children of men;' given it to mankind in common."

114. Sabine, *The Works of Gerrard Winstanley*, 251.

115. Sabine, *The Works of Gerrard Winstanley*, 260.

116. Sabine, *The Works of Gerrard Winstanley*, 260: "Ezek. 24.26, 27, &c. Jer. 33.7 to 12. Esay. 49.17, 18, &c. Zach. 8. from 4, to 12, Dan. 2.44, 45, Dan. 7.27. Hos. 14.5, 6,7. Joel 2.26, 27. Amos 9. from 8 to the end, Obad. 17.18.21. Mic. 5. from 7 to the end, Hab. 2.6, 7, 8, 13, 14. Gen. 18.18. Rom. 11.15. Zeph. 3. &c. Zech. 14.9."

117. Locke, *Two Treatises of Government*, §11, p. 104.

118. William Blackstone, cited by E. P. Thompson, *Customs in Common* (New Press, 1993), 162.

119. As Laura Brace observed, the "savage" in America and the poor in England are excluded from industriousness and rationality: Laura Brace, *The Politics of Property: Labour, Freedom and Belonging* (Edinburgh University Press, 2004), 35.

120. Sabine, *The Works of Gerrard Winstanley*, 269–77.

121. Locke, *Two Treatises of Government*, 19.

122. Locke, *Two Treatises of Government*, 25.

123. The relationship between right and obligation is not an opposition but, as my friend Anne Norton always reminded me during our conversations in Princeton, they refer to each other like the concave and the convex. Indeed, the deepest root of the term *ius* goes back to the verbal root "yeu," which means to unite and bind, and it is

the basis of both *ius* and "iungere" (to join together). If we accept this etymology, it follows that the most archaic layer of *ius* recalls the actions of joining and ob-ligare. See Benjamin García-Hernández, "La polisemia de *ius, iuris* ('derecho', 'aderezo') y la idea genuina ('unión') del Derecho Romano," *Revista de Estudios Latinos* 10 (2010): 29–47.

124. Rafe Blaufarb, *The Great Demarcation: The French Revolution and the Invention of Modern Property (Oxford University Press, 2016)*, 3.

125. Blaufarb, *The Great Demarcation*, 208; M. Waline, *L'individualisme et le droit* (Montchrestien, 1949), 334.

126. See Shael Herman, "The Uses and Abuses of Roman Law Texts," *American Journal of Comparative Law* 29, no. 4 (1981): 671–90; Thomas Rüfner, "The Roman Conception of Ownership and the Medieval Doctrine of Dominium," in *The Creation of the Ius Commune*, ed. John W. Cairns and Paul J. du Plessis (Edinburgh University Press, 2010), 127–42.

127. Robert Joseph Pothier, *Traité du droit de domaine de propriété* (Debure, 1772), 6.

128. Georg Friedrich Puchta, *Vorlesungen über das heutige römische Recht* (Leipzig, 1849), Bd. 1, 287. See Dieter Schwab, "Eigentum," in *Geschichtliche Grundbegriffe: Historisches Lexikon zur politisch-sozialen Sprache in Deutschland*, ed. Otto Brunner, Werner Conze, and Reinhart Koselleck (Klett-Cotta, 1992), 2:78.

129. Ludwig Arndts, *Lehrbuch der Pandekten* (Munchen, 1859), 191.

130. Karl Marx, *Capital* (Penguin, 1990), 1:286.

131. Marx, *Capital*, 1:283–86, 290.

132. Judith Butler's inquiry into Marx's *1844 Manuscripts* completely omits the analysis of property relations and their connection to estranged labor. As a result, it not only becomes unpolitical but also depoliticizes Marx's discourse on labor, capital, property, and the human-nature relationship. Judith Butler, "The Inorganic Body in the Early Marx: A Limit-Concept of Anthropocentrism," *Radical Philosophy* 2, no. 6 (2019): 3–17.

133. Butler, "The Inorganic Body in the Early Marx," 15.

134. Marx, *Capital*, 1:637–38; Karl Marx, *Capital* (Penguin, 1991), 3:949. See John Bellamy Foster, *Marx's Ecology (*Monthly Review Press, 2000); and Kohei Saito, *Karl Marx's Ecosocialism: Capital, Nature, and the Unfinished Critique of Political Economy (*Monthly Review Press, 2017).

135. Marx, *Capital*, 1:638.

136. Karl Marx, *Economic and Philosophical Manuscripts* (1844), in *Early Writings* (Penguin, 1992), 333.

137. Marx, *Economic and Philosophical Manuscripts*, 353.

138. Marx, *Capital*, 3:911.

139. Yan Thomas, "L'institution de la cité," *Le Débat* 74 (1993): 23–44.

3. DEMOCRACY AND THE DEMOCRATIC EXCESS

1. See European Commission for Democracy Through Law (Venice Commission), "Report on the Imperative Mandate and Similar Practices," Venice, June 12–13, 2009, http://www.venice.coe.int/webforms/documents/default.aspx?pdffile=CDL-AD(2009)027-e.

2. NCSL, "Recall of State Officials," September 15, 2001, https://www.ncsl.org/elections-and-campaigns/recall-of-state-officials.

3. Articles of Confederation, 1777, govinfo.gov, https://www.govinfo.gov/content/pkg/SMAN-107/pdf/SMAN-107-pg935.pdf.

4. Jonathan Elliot, ed., *Debates in the Several State Conventions, on the Adoption of the Federal Constitution, as Recommended by the General Convention at Philadelphia in 1787* (Philadelphia: J. B. Lippincott, 1891), 1:361.

5. The attempt to introduce the right to instruct representatives as an amendment to the Constitution was defeated forty-one to ten in the House of Representatives. See Thomas E. Cronin, *Direct Democracy: The Politics of Initiative, Referendum, and Recall* (Harvard University Press, 1989), 25; Joseph F. Zimmerman, *The Recall: Tribunal of the People* (SUNY Press, 2013).

6. Clara Egger and Raul-Magni Berton, "The Recall in France: A Long-Standing and Unresolved Debate," in *The Politics of Recall Elections*, ed. Janina Welp and Laurence Whitehead (Palgrave Macmillan, 2020), 60.

7. "L'appel des gilets jaunes de Commercy," December 2, 2018, https://manif-est.info/L-appel-des-gilets-jaunes-de-Commercy-853.html. See Stathis Kouvelakis, "The French Insurgency: Political Economy of the Gilets Jaunes," *New Left Review* 116/117 (2019): 75–96.

8. "Spain: The Podemos-IU Front of the Left," *Posadists Today*, June 17, 2016, http://posadiststoday.com/spain-the-podent-of-the-left/.

9. Giovanni Sartori, "La libertà degli eletti," *Corriere della sera*, April 13, 2013; Giovanni Sartori, "Una violazione macroscopica," *Corriere della sera*, November 6, 2013.

10. Michel Crozier, Samuel P. Huntington, and Joji Watanuki, *The Crisis of Democracy* (New York University Press, 1975), 113.

11. Crozier, Huntington, and Watanuki, *The Crisis of Democracy*, 147.

12. Kari Palonen, *The Politics of Limited Times. The Rhetoric of Temporal Judgment in Parliamentary Democracies* (Nomos, 2008), 18.

13. See Nadia Urbinati, "A Revolt Against Intermediary Bodies," *Constellation* 22, no. 4 (2015): 477–86.

14. Niccolò Machiavelli, *Discourses on Livy* (University of Chicago Press, 1996), 17.

15. Robespierre, June 14, 1793, in *Archives parlementaires de 1789 à 1860: Recueil complet des débats législatifs & politiques des Chambres françaises* (Paris:

Librairie administrative de P. Dupont, 1862–), 66:530, https://searchworks.stanford.edu/view/1071767.

16. Robespierre, June 14, 1793, in *Archives parlementaires*.

17. Olwen Hufton, "Women in Revolution, 1789–1796," *Past & Present* 53 (1971): 102.

18. Cronin, *Direct Democracy*, 18–19.

19. *The Records of the Federal Convention of 1787*, ed. Max Farrand (Yale University Press, 1911), 1:227.

20. *The Records of the Federal Convention of 1787*, *1:227*.

21. James Madison, *The Writings*, vol. 3, *1787*, ed. G. Hunt (G. P. Putnam's Sons, 1902), 125, 212.

22. Woody Holton, *Unruly Americans and the Origins of the Constitution* (Hill and Wang, 2007), 5, 14, 163. See also Woody Holton, "An 'Excess of Democracy'—or a Shortage?: The Federalists' Earliest Adversaries," *Journal of the Early Republic* 25, no. 3 (Fall 2005): 339–82.

23. Jacques Rancière, *Hatred of Democracy* (Verso, 2007), 38, 97. In this sense, Rancière speaks of a "démesure démocratique" that disrupts the partition of parts in order to extend equality.

24. Jacques Rancière and Alain Badiou, albeit with different emphasis, have accentuated the rarity of politics. For Rancière, it has to do with the action of a "part that has no part" that questions the partition of the whole. For Badiou, politics has the rarity of a truth-procedure that unfolds from a subjective truth in the name of what is right and interrupts the power of the state. What these two thinkers have in common is their difficulty, or impossibility, of conceiving the political event in the temporal dimension of duration. The time of politics remains that of disruption.

25. See Condorcet, *Selected Writings*, ed. Keith Michael Baker (Bobbs-Merril, 1976), 150–51. Lucien Jaume, "La souveraineté montagnarde: République, peuple et territoire," in *La Constitution du 24 Juin 1793: L'utopie dans le droit public français?*, ed. Jean Bart et al. (Editions Universitaires de Dijon, 1997), 119–20.

26. Condorcet, in *Archives Parlementaires*, February 15, 1793, 58:601.

27. Hannah Arendt, "Civil Disobedience," in *Crises of the Republic* (Harvest, 1972), 83: It "would be an event of great significance to find a constitutional niche for civil disobedience."

28. Carl Schmitt, *Constitutional Theory* (Duke University Press, 2008), 251. I will return to this later in this chapter.

29. Alexis de Tocqueville, *The Recollections* (New York: McMillan, 1896), 98.

30. de Tocqueville, *The Recollections, 98*.

31. See Joan Wallach Scott, *Sex and Secularism (Princeton University Press, 2017)*, 63–66.

32. Darline G. Levy and Harriet B. Applewhite, "Women and Militant Citizenship in

Revolutionary Paris," in *Rebel Daughters: Women and French Revolution*, ed. Sara E. Melzer and Leslie W. Rabine (Oxford University Press, 1992), 88–89.

33. See Linda Zerilli, "Feminist Theory and the Canon of Political Thought," in *The Oxford Handbook of Political Theory*, ed. John S. Dryzek, Bonnie Honig, and Anne Phillips (Oxford University Press, 2006), 108.

34. Edith Thomas, *The Women Incendiaries* (Haymarket, 2007), 172.

35. David Barry, *Women and Political Insurgency* (University of Durham Press, 1996), 148.

36. See Vincenzo Ruggiero, *Understanding Political Violence: A Criminological Analysis* (Open University Press, 2006), 40–41.

37. Thomas, *The Women Incendiaries*, 178.

38. See Welp and Whitehead, eds., *The Politics of Recall Elections*; Laurence Morel and Matt Quortrup, *The Routledge Handbook to Referendum and Direct Democracy* (Routledge, 2018); Saskia P. Ruth, Yanina Welp, and Laurence Whitehead, *Let the People Rule? Direct Democracy in the Twenty-First Century* (ECPR, 2017); Marc Van der Hulst, *The Parliamentary Mandate: A Global Comparative Study* (Inter-Parliamentary Union, 2000).

39. Gurevitch provides a picture of this pluralistic society: "From top to bottom medieval society is corporate. Associations of vassals, knightly orders, monastic brotherhoods and Catholic clergy; town communes, merchant and trade guilds; defensive unions, religious brotherhoods; village communities, kindreds, patriarchal and individual family groupings—these and similar collectives spliced individuals together in closely knit microcosms which gave protection and help, and which were built up on a basis of mutual exchange of services and support." A. J. Gurevitch, *Categories of Medieval Culture* (Routledge & Kegan Paul, 1985), 187.

40. Brunner wrote that a feud could be understood as a war "conducted against one's lord with the assistance of foreign powers." He continued, "Such actions are incomprehensible from the perspective of modern constitutional or international law, where they can appear only as gross violations of national and international law, as high treason, as violent interference in the internal affairs of a state by foreign powers. In the Middle Ages, however, we see rulers and subjects declare war and conclude peace with each other 'as if' each were subject to international law." Otto Brunner, *Land and Lordship: Structures of Governance in Medieval Austria* (University of Pennsylvania Press, 1992), 14. These categories, Brunner concluded, are "inapplicable to the Middle Ages, where neither the sovereign state nor international law existed in the modern sense" (34).

41. Martyn Rady, *Nobility, Land, and Service in Medieval Hungary* (Palgrave Macmillan, 2001), 173.

42. Alice M. Holden, "The Imperative Mandate in the Spanish Cortes of the Middle Ages," *American Political Science Review* 24, no. 4 (1930): 897.

43. Ch. Müller, *Das imperative und freie Mandat* (A. W. Sijthoff, 1966), 161–204; H. Triepel, *Delegation und Mandat im Öffentlichen Recht. Eine kritische Studie* (W. Kohlhammer Verlag, 1942).

44. Holden, "The Imperative Mandate," 900.

45. Johannes Althusius, *Politica* (Liberty Fund, 1995), XVIII, §66; Thomas O. Hueglin, *Early Modern Concepts for a Late Modern World: Althusius on Community and Federalism* (Wilfrid Laurier University Press, 1999), 149.

46. Edmund Burke, *Miscellaneous Writings* (Liberty Fund, 1999), 4:11–12; my emphasis.

47. Müller, *Das imperative*, 141.

48. European Commission for Democracy Through Law (Venice Commission), "Report on the Imperative Mandate and Similar Practices," Art. 5.

49. Emile Durkheim, *Professional Ethics and Civic Morals* (Routledge, 2003), 91–92.

50. Carl Schmitt, *Constitutional Theory* (Duke University Press, 2008), 289.

51. Schmitt, *Constitutional Theory*, 289.

52. Schmitt, *Constitutional Theory*, 251.

53. Thomas Hobbes, *Leviathan* (Oxford University Press, 1998), 109.

54. Locke, *Second Treatise*, §89; my emphasis.

55. Carl Schmitt, *Political Theology* (University of Chicago Press, 2005), 36.

56. Schmitt, *Constitutional Theory*, 243. See also Gerhard Leibholz, *Strukturprobleme der moderne Demokratie* (Verlag C. F. Müller, 1958).

57. Rafe Blaufarb, *The Great Demarcation: The French Revolution and the Invention of Modern Property (Oxford University Press, 2016)*, 52.

58. Jean-Joseph Mounier, who was among those who wrote the draft declaration of the demarcation outlined on August 4, 1789, made explicit that "the principle of all sovereignty resides in the nation, and no corps, no individual can have an authority which does not emanate expressly from it." Blaufarb, *The Great Demarcation*, 52.

59. Jon Elster, "The Night of August 4, 1789: A Study of Social Interaction in Collective Decision Making," in *Revue Européenne des Sciences Sociales* 45, no. 136 (2007): 76–77.

60. James Harvey Robinson, *Readings in European History* (Ginn and Co., 1904), 2:404–5.

61. Silvia Marzagalli, "Economic and Demographic Developments," in *The Oxford Handbook of the French Revolution*, ed. David Andress (Oxford University Press, 2015), 13.

62. Eugen Weber, *Peasants Into Frenchmen: The Modernization of Rural France, 1870–1914* (Stanford University Press, 1976), 58.

63. Ch. Müller, *Das imperative und freie Mandat* (A. W. Sijthoff, 1966), 32–50.

64. "Sa Majesté déclare que dans les tenues suivantes des États généraux elle

ne souffrira pas que les cahiers ou mandats puissent être jamais considérés comme impératifs: ils ne doivent être que des simples instructions confiées à la conscience et à la libre opinion des députés dont on aura fait choix." Philippe-Joseph-Benjamin Buchez and Prosper Charles Roux, eds., *Histoire parlementaire de la révolution française* (Paris: Pauline Libraire, 1884), 2:14.

65. Alexis de Tocqueville, *The Ancient Régime and the French Revolution* (University Press, 2011), 61, 183.

66. Keith Michael Baker, *Inventing the French Revolution* (Cambridge University Press, 1994), 249.

67. "Projet de Déclaration des droits naturels, civils et politiques des hommes," in *Oeuvres de Condorcet* (Paris: Firmin Didot Frères Libraires, 1847), art. 25–28, 12:276–77.

68. P.-J. Buchez and P. C. Roux, *Histoire parlementaire de la Révolution française* (Paris, 1834–1838), 10:194; trans. John Hall Stewart, *A Documentary Survey of the French Revolution* (: Macmillan, 1951), 165–66.

69. Le Chapelier Law (June 14, 1791), in Stewart, *A Documentary Survey of the French Revolution*, 165–66, https://revolution.chnm.org/items/show/480.

70. Buchez and Roux, *Histoire parlementaire de la Révolution française*, 10:194; Stewart, *A Documentary Survey of the French Revolution*, 165–66; my emphasis.

71. Jean Varlet, "Proposal for a Special and Imperative Mandate" (1792), in *Social and Political Thought of the French Revolution* (Peter Lang, 2001), 154.

72. Varlet, "Proposal for a Special and Imperative Mandate," 154.

73. Lucien Jaume, *Le discours jacobin et la démocratie* (Fayard, 1989), 289.

74. David Gilles, "Représentation et souveraineté chez les enragés (1792–1794)," in *Le concept de Représentation dans la pensée politique: Actes du colloque d'Aix-en-Provence (May 2002)* (Presses Universitaires d'Aix-Marseille, 2003), 253–86.

75. *Le Cri du Peuple* 26 (March 27, 1871).

76. "Surprisingly," writes Wolin, "despite the attenuation of democracy at the level of national politics, there still exists a highly flourishing archaic political culture that is democratic, participatory, localist, and, overall, more egalitarian than elitist in ideology." Sheldon S. Wolin, The Presence of the Past: Essay on the State and the Constitution (Johns Hopkins University Press, 1989), 81.

77. It seems to me this is also the limit of the left populism described by Chantal Mouffe. Through a strategy of construction of a "political frontier," Mouffe points out the possibility of restoring the agonistic character of democracy, recovering and radicalizing democratic institutions, after and against the neoliberal political regression of postdemocracy. Chantal Mouffe, *For a Left Populism* (Verso, 2018).

78. Jean-Jacques Rousseau, *Politics and the Arts* (Cornell University Press, 1960), 125–26.

79. *Los Angeles Times*, September 10, 1911.

80. Peter Viereck, "Vox Populi—Vox Dei or Vox Diaboli? The Dangers of Direct Democracy," *Southwest Review* 41, no. 2 (1956): 113–24.

81. For more on this, see Anne Norton's forthcoming work *Anarchy, Courage, Democracy*. The stimulating, thought-provoking conversations with Anne during our stay in Princeton were precious in reworking this chapter. These conversations often took place during the numerous dinners that made the long year of isolation caused by the pandemic humanly bearable.

82. Rod Farmer, "The Power to the People: The Progressive Movement for the Recall," *New England Journal of History* 57, no. 2 (2001): 64; William Bennett Munro, *The Initiative Referendum and Recall* (D. Appleton and Co., 1915), 42.

83. Cronin, *Direct Democracy*, 125. The possibility to recall elected representatives, which is actually forbidden in many modern constitutions, exists, usually through referendum, in some countries, such as Venezuela, Nigeria, and Switzerland in six of its cantons.

84. Ellis Paxson Oberholtzer, *The Referendum in America* (New York: Charles Scribner's Sons, 1900), 343.

85. The Populist Party Platform (Omaha, 1892) reads: "We seek to restore the government of the Republic to the hands of 'the plain people,' with which class it originated. . . . We commend to the favorable consideration of the people and the reform press the legislative system known as the initiative and referendum. . . . We favor a constitutional provision limiting the office of President and Vice-President to one term, and providing for the election of Senators of the United States by a direct vote of the people." George Brown Tindall, ed., *A Populist Reader: Selections from the Works of American Populist Leaders* (Harper & Row, 1966), 90–96.

86. *The Coming Nation*, July 11, 1896.

87. Oberholtzer, *The Referendum in America*, ix.

88. Antonio Gramsci, *Selections from Political Writings, 1921–1926* (Lawrence & Wishart, 1978), 50.

89. Schmitt, *Constitutional Theory*, 305. In relation to the members of the public, in 1927, Walter Lippmann observed that "in governing the work of other men by votes or by the expression of opinion they can only reward or punish a result, accept or reject alternatives presented to them. They can say yes or no to something which has been done, yes or no to a proposal, but they cannot create, administer and actually perform the act they have in mind. . . . To the realm of executive acts, each of us, as a member of the public, remains always external." Walter Lippmann, *The Phantom Public* (Transaction, 1993), 42.

90. Carl Schmitt, *Volksentscheid und Volksbegehren* (Walter de Gruyter & Co., 1927), 32–36.

91. Schmitt, *Volksentscheid und Volksbegehren*, 49.

92. Cronin, *Direct Democracy*, 243.

93. On the incompatibility of the imperative mandate and modern democracy, see also Ernst-Wolfgang Böckenförde, "Mittelbare/repräsentative Demokratie als eigentliche Form der Demokratie. Bemerkungen zu Begriff und Verwirklichungsproblem der Demokratie als Staats- und Regierungsform," in *Staatsorganisation und Staatsfunktionen im Wandel, Festschrift für Kurt Eichenberger zum 60*, ed. G. Müller et al. (Verlag Helbig & Lichtenhahn, 1982), 301–28.

94. Landauer, "The United Republics of Germany and Their Constitution," 200–1.

95. Landauer, "The United Republics of Germany and Their Constitution," 200–1.

96. Schmitt, *Constitutional Theory*, 289.

97. Schmitt, *Constitutional Theory*, 289: "An imperative mandate of the medieval style, however, which involves dependence of a deputy on instructions and directions by an estate, other types of organization, or by parties, contradicts the idea of political unity as well as the fundamental presupposition of democracy, in particular of the substantive homogeneity of a people, whose natural and political unity is considered identical."

98. See Chapter 2.

99. Madison, *The Writings*, 3:78, 213.

100. Schmitt, *Constitutional Theory*, 289.

4. CITIZENSHIP AND SANCTUARY

1. Major David Wise, *The Role of Sanctuary in an Insurgency* (School of Advanced Military Studies [SAMS]), 2008.

2. Wise, *The Role of Sanctuary in an Insurgency*, 49.

3. Wise, *The Role of Sanctuary in an Insurgency*, 50.

4. Wise, *The Role of Sanctuary in an Insurgency*, 28.

5. Obiora Chinedu Okafor, *Refugee Law After 9/11: Sanctuary and Security in Canada and the United States* (UBC Press, 2020).

6. Norman M. Trenholme, *The Right of Sanctuary in England* (University of Missouri, 1903), 91n14.

7. Trenholme, *The Right of Sanctuary*, 86. William Chester Jordan, "A Fresh Look at Medieval Sanctuary," in *Law and the Illicit in Medieval Europe*, ed. R. Mazo Karras, J. Kaye, and E. A. Matter (University of Pennsylvania Press, 2008), 21.

8. Trenholme, *The Right to Sanctuary*, 91.

9. Gervase Rosser, "Sanctuary and Social Negotiation in Medieval England" in *The Cloister and the World*, ed. J. Blair and B. Golding (Clarendon, 1996), 60.

10. Rosser, "Sanctuary and Social Negotiation in Medieval England," 61. Other examples are found in Margaret Mead's study of Papua New Guinea: "In a primitive community, sanctuary and hospitality are so intermixed that it is difficult to distinguish between them." Margaret Mead, *New Lives for Old: Cultural Transformation—Manus 1928–1953* (Morrow, 1956), 315. Or, in relation to India,

Westermarck wrote: "Among the Kafirs of the Hindu-Kush there are several 'cities of
refuge,' the largest being the village of Mergron, which is almost entirely peopled
by . . . descendants of persons who have slain some fellow-tribesman." Edward Westermarck, "Asylum," in *Encyclopedia of Religion and Ethics*, ed. J. Hastings (T&T Clark,
1909), 161. Other examples: Linda Rabben, *Sanctuary and Asylum: A Social and
Political History* (University of Washington Press, 2016), 34–36.

11. See A. P. Stanley, *Historical Memorials of Westminster Abbey* (London, 1876),
379: "The Sanctuaries of medieval Christendom may have been necessary remedies
for a barbarous state of society; but when the barbarism of which they formed a part
disappeared, they became almost unmixed evils."

12. Katharyne Mitchell and Key MacFarlane, *The Sanctuary Network: Transnational Church Activism and Refugee Protection in Europe*, in *Handbook on Critical
Geographies of Migration*, ed. K. Mitchell, R. Jones, and J. Fluri (Edward Elgar,
2019), 416.

13. John T. Noonan Jr., "Foreword," in Ignatius Bau, *This Ground Is Holy: Church
Sanctuary and Central American Refugees* (Paulist, 1985), 2.

14. "Elie Wiesel, noted Jewish author and survivor of the Holocaust . . . castigated
those who used the term 'illegal alien,' calling it an 'antinomy' and asking rhetori-
cally, 'How can a human being be illegal?'. . . He declared that all human beings
are dwellings of God and therefore sacred and inviolable." Bau, *This Ground Is
Holy*, 22.

15. Referring only to "civilized" Europe and the United States, "From 2013 to
September 30, 2019, over 19,000 migrants died and were missing in the waters of the
Mediterranean Sea in an attempt to reach Europe." "Dal 2013 al 2019 oltre 19 mila
migranti morti nel Mediterraneo," *Vita*, October 3, 2019, http://www.vita.it/it/article
/2019/10/03/dal-2013-al-2019-oltre-19-mila-migranti-morti-nel-mediterraneo/152848/.
At least 7,000 migrants have died along the US-Mexico border since 1998: Samuel Gil-
bert, "2020 Was Deadliest Year for Migrants Crossing Unlawfully Into US Via Arizona,"
Guardian, January 30, 2021, https://www.theguardian.com/us-news/2021/jan/30/us
-mexico-border-crossings-arizona-2020-deadliest-year.

16. Isabel Kershner, "Pardon Plea by Adolf Eichmann, Nazi War Criminal, Is Made
Public," *New York Times*, January 27, 2016, http://www.nytimes.com/2016/01/28
/world/middleeast/israel-adolf-eichmann-holocaust.html.

17. Bau, *The Ground Is Holy*, 181.

18. Peter H. Schuck, "The Transformation of Immigration Law," *Columbia Law
Review* 84, no. 1 (1984): 81. The text reads as follows: "If that is so, the collapse of
immigration enforcement may actually generate a profound public reaction against
aliens and the communitarian values that increasingly protect them, reviving the nativ-
ist impulses that have always been an important, albeit often deplorable, element of
our national character."

19. Jim Corbett, from an unpublished paper titled "Sanctuary and the Covenant Community," cited in Bau, *This Ground Is Holy*, 21.

20. Hannah Arendt, *The Origins of Totalitarianism* (Harvest, 1973), 296; Seyla Benhabib, *The Rights of the Others: Aliens, Residents, and Citizens* (Cambridge University Press, 2004), 49–70.

21. W. E. B. Du Bois, *Black Reconstruction in America, 1860–1880* (Meridian, 1964), 700.

22. Mary McThomas, *Performing Citizenship: Undocumented Migrants in the United States* (Routledge, 2018).

23. Carole Pateman, *The Problem of Political Obligations: A Critique of Liberal Theory* (University of California Press, 1985), 174.

24. Santi Romano, *L'ordinamento Giuridico. Studi sul Concetto, le Fonti e I Caratteri del Diritto* (Tipografia Editrice Cav. Mariotti, 1917), 42.

25. Randy Lippert, "Sanctuary Practices, Rationalities, and Sovereignties," *Alternatives* 29 (2005): 535–55.

26. Hiroshi Oda, "Ethnography of Relationship Among Church Sanctuary Actors in Germany," in *Sanctuary Practices in International Perspectives*, ed. R. K. Lippert and S. Rehaag (Routledge, 2013), 155.

27. Oda, "Ethnography of Relationship Among Church Sanctuary Actors in Germany," 155.

28. Joan Scott, *Sex and Secularism* (Princeton University Press, 2017).

29. Cesare Beccaria, *On Crimes and Punishments and Other Writings* (Cambridge University Press, 1995), 92.

30. Beccaria, *On Crimes and Punishments and Other Writings*, 92.

31. *US v. Aguilar*, official trial transcript, 1986, no. CR-85–008-PHX-EHC (D. Ariz), cited in Susan B. Coutin, "Smugglers or Samaritans in Tucson, Arizona: Producing and Contesting Legal Truth," *American Ethnologist* 22, no. 3 (1995): 556.

32. Beccaria, *On Crimes and Punishments*, 92.

33. *US v. Aguilar*, cited in Coutin, *Smugglers or Samaritans in Tucson*, 558.

34. Pierre Lascoumes, "L'illégalisme, outil d'analyse," *Sociétés et Représentation* 3 (1996): 78–84.

35. Michel Foucault, *Discipline and Punish: The Birth of the Prison* (Vintage, 1995), 274.

36. *US v. Aguilar*, cited in Coutin, *Smugglers or Samaritans in Tucson*, 557.

37. Coutin, *Smugglers or Samaritans in Tucson*, 553.

38. John Stephens, "About Civil Initiative," 2009, https://designop.us/wrote/about-civil-initiative.

39. Jim Corbett, "Sanctuary, Basic Rights, and Humanity's Fault Lines," 1987, http://weberstudies.weber.edu/archive/archive%20A%20%20Vol.%201-10.3/Vol.%205.1/5.1Corbet.htm.

40. Jim Corbett, *Goatwalking* (Vicking, 1991), 106.

41. New Sanctuary Movement of Philadelphia, "Who We Are," https://www
.sanctuaryphiladelphia.org/who-we-are/.

42. "No city, constitution or individual man will ever become perfect unless some
chance event compels those few philosophers who aren't vicious (the ones who are
now called useless) to take charge of a city whether they want to or not, and compels
the city to obey them, or until a god inspires the present rulers and kings or their off-
spring with a true erotic love of true philosophy." Plato, *Republic* 499b, in *Complete
Works of Plato*, ed. John Cooper (Hackett, 1997), 1120.

43. Plato, *Republic* 500c–d, in *Complete Works of Plato*, 1122.

44. Plato, *Letter VII* 328c, in *Complete Works of Plato*, 1649.

45. Hilary Cunningham, "The Emergence of the Ontario Sanctuary Coalition: From
Humanitarian and Compassionate Review to Civil Initiative," in Lippert and Rehaag,
eds., *Sanctuary Practices*, 172.

46. My memory goes to my friend, the philosopher and Jesuit Giuseppe Pirola,
who invited me to reflect on the political implications—not only the religious ones—
of the distinction between friends, on the one hand, and brothers and sisters, on the
other.

47. See Loukia Kotronaki, "Outside the Doors: Refugee Accommodation Squats
and Heterotopy Politics," *South Atlantic Quarterly* 117, no. 3 (2018): 914–24, who
views the City Plaza experiment in Greece as a laboratory for new forms of citizenship and collective identity. See also Olga Lafazani, "Homeplace Plaza: Challenging
the Border Between Host and Hosted," *South Atlantic Quarterly* 117, no. 3 (2018):
897–904.

48. Reverend William Sloane Coffin Jr., cited in Philip Marfleet, "Understanding
'Sanctuary': Faith and Traditions of Asylum," *Journal of Refugee Studies* 24, no. 3
(2011): 450.

49. Myriam Revault d'Allonnes, *Le pouvoir des commencements. Essai sur
l'autorité* (Seuil, 2006), 13.

50. Jordan, "A Fresh Look at Medieval Sanctuary," 19.

51. Trenholme, *The Right of Sanctuary in England*, 30.

52. Krista Kesselring, "Abjuration and Its Demise: The Changing Face of Royal
Justice in the Tudor Period," *Canadian Journal of History* 34 (1999): 353.

53. Kesselring, "Abjuration and Its Demise," 346.

54. Paolo Prodi, *Una storia della giustizia. Dal pluralism dei fori al modern
dualismo tra coscienza e diritto* (Il Mulino, 2000).

55. Trenholme, *The Right to Sanctuary in England*, 31.

56. James R. Hertzler, "The Abuse and Outlawing of Sanctuary for Debt in
Seventeenth-Century England," *Historical Journal* 14, no. 3 (1971): 467–77.

57. Riot Act (1714–1715), https://www.gutenberg.org/files/8142/8142-h/8142-h.htm.

58. T. B. Macaulay, *The History of England from the Accession of James the Second* (1st ed., London, 1848; MAS Press, 1968), 1:345.

59. See Rosser, "Sanctuary and Social Negotiation in Medieval England," 76.

60. Macaulay, *The History of England*, 345–47.

61. Macaulay, *The History of England*, 345.

62. Romano, *L'ordinamento Giuridico*, 42.

63. Macaulay, *The History of England*, 345–47.

64. Kesselring, "Abjuration and Its Demise," 351.

65. From 1718 to 1775, approximately fifty thousand people convicted of noncapital felonies against property were transported from England to America, one-quarter of all British immigrants to colonial America during this century. The prisoners were sold as indentured servants in the "extremely lucrative business" that began with the 1718 Transportation Act. Javier Bleichmar, "Deportation as Punishment: A Historical Analysis of the British Practice of Banishment and Its Impact on Modern Constitutional Law," *Georgetown Immigration Law Journal* 14 (1999–2000): 124–28. The 1718 Transportation Act, by promising relief from robbery and other felonies, provided both a cheap labor force in the colonies and a generalized course on the discipline of the new private property regime.

66. "Nonetheless, so much virtue emerged in some of the new cities and empires that arose among the Roman ruins that, even if one did not dominate the others, they were nonetheless harmonious and ordered together so that they freed Italy and defended it from the barbarians." Niccolò Machiavelli, *Florentine Histories* (Princeton University Press, 1988), book V.1, 185–86.

67. Karl Shoemaker, "Sanctuary for Crime in Early Common Law," in Lippert and Rehaag, eds., *Sanctuary Practices*, 22.

68. Karl Shoemaker, *Sanctuary and Crime in the Middle Ages, 400–1500* (Fordham University Press, 2011), 31–35.

69. Shoemaker, *Sanctuary and Crime in the Middle Ages*, 123.

70. Lia Haro and Ronald Coles, "Reimagining Fugitive Democracy and Transformative Sanctuary with Vlack Frontline Communities in the Underground Railroad," *Political Theory* (2019): 1–28.

71. Sheldon S. Wolin, *The Presence of the Past: Essay on the State and the Constitution* (Johns Hopkins University Press, 1989), 81.

72. New Sanctuary Movement of Philadelphia, "Who We Are."

INDEX

Massimiliano Tomba is Professor in the Department of History of Consciousness at the University of California, Santa Cruz. He is the author of *Insurgent Universality: An Alternative Legacy of Modernity* (2019, co-winner, David and Elaine Spitz Prize), *Attraverso la piccolo porta: Quattro studi su Walter Benjamin* (2017), *Marx's Temporalities* (2012), *La vera politica: Kant e Benjamin* (2006), and *Krise und Kritik bei Bruno Bauer. Kategorien des Politischen im nachhegelschen Denken* (2005).

www.ingramcontent.com/pod-product-compliance
Lightning Source LLC
Chambersburg PA
CBHW031153020426
42333CB00013B/647